The Porcelain Doll

Desislava Kaludova

Dedicated to
my mother Penka,
my father Stoyan,
my aunt Angelina,
and my grandparents,
Iovka, Dimo, Domna and Ivan.

*"We are products of our past,
but we don't have to be prisoners of it."*

— Rick Warren, from *The Purpose-Driven Life: What on Earth Am I Here For?* Rick Warren is an American Baptist Evangelical Christian pastor and author.

Acknowledgments

I owe thanks to many people for the creation of this book.

First, I owe huge appreciation to my mother, for her emotional and financial investments in my education over my lifetime; and for the passion of reading and writing that I inherited from her.

Also, I am forever indebted to my husband, Georgi, for his constant support through my various endeavors in life, including writing this book. He survived, without complaining, my almost total immersion in the creation of this book.

Many thanks to Janet Long for introducing me to my editor, Linda Jay.

Great appreciation to Linda Jay for her many editorial talents and her sharp eye for mistakes. She shaped the final text of the book. It was not an easy task to correct my imperfections. I might have been writing in English, but some of my sentences still sounded like they were written in Bulgarian, my native language, until she started her job.

Profound gratitude to all my teachers from VIII School. "A. S. Pushkin" in Varna, Bulgaria, who cultivated in me the love for literature and writing during all my years of studying there.

Thanks to my friend Silvia Kusminova, who translated into German some of the sentences I used in the first part of the book.

Thank you, Donika Drentcheva, for organizing my attendance at the book signing event for Isabel Allende's book *The Long Petal of the Sea*. I was so impressed by that event, which undoubtedly had a strong influence on me for starting to write *The Porcelain Doll*. Thanks to Rositsa Penkova, for giving me valuable advice about getting accepted into the Journalism Program at Sofia University.

Thanks to Tanya Kostova, for her help on translating the Bulgarian wedding song.

Thank you to all my family members and friends who were faithful readers and thoughtfully critiqued the draft of *The Porcelain Doll*. Bless you all!

Author's Note

Writing books was what I always envisioned myself doing, since I first learned how to read and write. God, however, had a different plan for me and put my life on a divergent path. I spent most of my life studying and working in the medical field. Now, during this time of the pandemic, He blessed me with an unexpected opportunity to fulfill my childhood dream of writing a book. As Chekhov once said, "Medicine is my lawful wife; literature is my mistress."

I never imagined that my first book would be written in English. I assumed that writing in a language that is not my native language would be challenging. But here I was one day, and without any previous plan, I started writing in my notebook at work, in English. I never expected how much I would enjoy this process. Still, while I was writing, I encountered periods when the task seemed so overwhelming, I doubted both myself and my ability to finish the book.

"I gather together the dreams, fantasies, and experiences that preoccupied me as a girl, that stay with me and appear and reappear in different shapes and forms in all my work. Without telling everything that happened, they document all that remains most vivid." –Bell Hooks (Bell Hooks is the pen name of Gloria Jean Watkins, an American author, feminist and social activist).

I did not intend this book to be a memoir. It was originally designed to describe some episodes from my early life. Some events were omitted in the story, while others have been changed in order to make the book appeal to a broader public. Although people might think they recognize themselves in my characters, it is important to note that the characters are purely fictional creations. I know that many of my relatives and friends who are not mentioned in the book will be disappointed. To them, I now make a promise that, if God's will and my health allow me to continue writing books, those relatives and friends will be in the center of the stories in my subsequent books.

Some of my relatives' names have been changed; and most of the new names have symbolic meanings. For example, Rose's name was created after the famous flower that is a symbol of Bulgaria. My father took his name after his grandfather—Miho. That way I wanted to broaden the story to include more of the family members and my family history without telling it all. The places highlighted, and their geographical descriptions, are real.

In this book there are many fondly remembered tales and proverbs that I heard as a child from my parents and grandparents. I also describe stories that I have not personally experienced myself. Instead, they actually happened to my friends, sisters, cousins, daughter and husband.

My desire was that my heroine Gabriella and her life would represent all the prematurely born children that modern medicine has been able to save. Also, I wanted Rose's character to be a portrait, not only of my mother Penka, but also of all the other mothers who struggled and fought for their children who had difficulty coming into this world.

The characters in my book live during a very intense historical period. In these years, between September 1944 and November 1989, of autocratic regime in Bulgaria, the members of the government who were leaders of the Communist party were not interested in personal stories, only in benefits for all or part of society.

By contrast, I wanted my story to be deeply personal. I wanted to show how historical events affected the lives of ordinary Bulgarians.

I wished to describe some Bulgarian traditions, beliefs, superstitions, and proverbs in an interesting and memorable way to readers who knew nothing about my native country. By all means, however, this book is not a guide in ethnology. One of my favorite chapters, though, is the one in which I describe the modern version of a typical Bulgarian wedding (Part III, Chapter 7, "The Wedding"). I hope you will enjoy reading this chapter as much as I did writing it. I am happy that these traditions are not forgotten; many young people nowadays are keeping them alive.

My female characters are experienced cooks, just as their mothers and grandmothers were. Although I mention briefly some traditional Bulgarian dishes in the book, my goal was not to describe in depth the typical Bulgarian kitchen. My mother's culinary book *Let the Soul Partake of the Delight* has been my model for years, and is the guideline that I follow for cooking. It is available to anyone who has a sincere interest in Bulgarian culinary art. The book was published in 2001 by the publisher Slavena in Bulgarian, English and German.

This book is also dedicated to the peers of my generation, born in the late 1960s–1970s. We were children who grew up under the Communist regime, and who had survived the changes and the uncertainties of the transition period (after November 1989); we often left our country in hopes of a better life. A significant number of my classmates and friends now live all over the world. The umbilical cord that connects us, however, as people who live abroad from our Motherland, will never be severed.

On the other hand, after living for decades in the USA, or in other parts of the world, we eventually become an integral part of our new countries. We have learned about the history, and have accepted the values of, our adopted nations. I truly relished writing this part of the book, in which Gabby lives in United States. The adaptation period was difficult, but it was worth it to both my heroine and to me personally. My friends and I encountered different situations, made new friends and discovered that we possess more strength that we had initially thought.

The quotations in Part I are from my daily calendar at work, *"A Year of Daily Wisdom,"* by Marianne Williamson. I found this calendar on my desk when I started working as a Registered Nurse. Although I did not know whom the book belonged to, I have been reading the inspirations religiously, every morning before work, for the past five years. They have definitely become an important part of my life, and ended up in my book.

Contents

PART I

1

The Little Tinker Bell Was Born

"No sickness can diminish our capacity to love."

– Marianne Williamson, "A Year of Daily Wisdom."

Long, long ago in a faraway land, a little girl was born. No, this is not a fairy-tale story, even if the girl looked like Tinker Bell. Her tiny little fingers and toes were so adorable, her Mom could not stop kissing them. However, the doctors had delicately told Rose, the little girl's mother, that her baby, who was born prematurely about a month earlier, probably would not survive long.

Rose was young and inexperienced as a mother, so she did not know enough to worry very much. She had grown up in a Communist country where she was not allowed to believe in God, and never learned how to pray. Prayer was, in fact, all she needed now. But she did believe in fairy tales.

On this cold but sunny February morning, Rose was sitting comfortably in a recliner in the bright, warm hospital room, located in the sheltered hallway of the big hospital on the outskirts of town. This wing belonged to the pediatric unit for premature babies. The young blond German nurse on the morning shift gave the little baby to Rose, to hold and nurse. Nurse's blue eyes were a striking contrast to the deep brown eyes of the tiny baby Rose was holding closely to her own heart.

Rose was kissing her baby's fingers and toes as the baby made funny facial expressions and wrinkled her tiny nose. Rose and her husband had not yet decided on a name for the tiny girl. They were not sure if they should choose a traditional Bulgarian name, or a modern name. Rose wondered if it was worth even thinking about a name for their daughter, who might not survive long. Rose felt the warmth of tears sliding down her pretty young face. No, she had promised herself she was not going to cry today. After all, she needed to be strong for her daughter. This baby is absolutely going to survive. Rose and her husband will eventually take their daughter back to their native country, Bulgaria, where she will be able to see her grandparents, who are very excited to meet her. Their daughter will grow up to be a strong and smart woman.

The blond nurse (why could Rose not remember the nurse's name?) motioned to the mother that it was time to put the baby back into the incubator. Rose gently placed her daughter inside, on her back, and closed the side openings of the machine. The baby looked even smaller now, lying alone inside this big, scary incubator. But it was there, of course, to keep her alive. Rose waved good-bye to her little Tinker Bell. The young mother felt tears starting to fall again. *"No, I am not going to cry today,"* she thought to herself.

Rose felt that she needed to take a walk before she could go back home to her husband. The dry, cold northern air, which burned her beautiful young face, made her cheeks pink from the cold, but at least her head cleared.

Rose decided to stroll along the main street of the little town, enjoying the view of the beautiful stores with their inviting, glittering showcases. These were so different from the empty, gloomy store windows of her native country, Bulgaria. Although Rose and her husband had been living in this small Eastern German town for about six months already, she still felt stricken by the beauty and abundance in the clothing and food stores. She even found her favorite fruits, oranges, available in Bulgaria only in limited quantities, right before New Year's Day. During her unexpected pregnancy, Rose had developed a strong craving for those oranges.

During her morning walk, Rose suddenly saw a little store, painted in blue-and-white colors. She hadn't paid attention to its existence during her previous walks. On the door was the sign "Geöffnet" (Open). The store was open at this early hour and for some reason, that made Rose's heart sing. As she stepped inside, an old, friendly lady dressed in pink clothes greeted her warmly. Rose could not help but compare her bright outfit to the dark, mostly black clothes that older women in Bulgaria wore.

Even Rose's own mother, who was far from being elderly, started dressing only in dark clothes after she turned forty. This was the custom in the country—older women dressed in black, looking like they were in perpetual mourning for their deceased relatives. Rose quickly shook her head to clear out negative thoughts. No, today is a sunny, happy day! Her little girl is about one month old, and is surviving—despite all the odds. Rose will not be sad and think about death. She will not let her worries about her precious baby, and her constant homesickness, affect her today.

The pink-clothed lady started chattering quickly in German, while Rose just smiled shyly. She was able to understand only half of what the lady said. The old woman somehow sensed that the young one was a foreigner far away from her family, hugged Rose and offered her coffee. This behavior was unusual for a cold German nature, or so Rose was told by the people who had lived in this country longer than she and were more familiar with this matter. Rose smiled widely and accepted the cup of coffee. Drinking the rich black drink had become her habit, and a little refuge in Germany. On this cold morning, the coffee felt like a warm elixir going through her veins.

Rose was gracefully walking around the store, drinking her coffee, gazing at the clothes and souvenirs. Suddenly, she stopped and moved closer to the window's showcase. How did she not notice this doll earlier when she had looked at the store from the street?! Rose's elegant hand held a little porcelain doll, painted in blue, red and white. The figurine was delicate, just like Rose's little girl, who was waiting for her mother's next morning visit in the hospital. Surprisingly for a German doll, this little beauty had deep, dark eyes. "Wieviel kostet es?" ("How much does it cost?") Rose asked the pink lady, proud of her improving German language skills.

The lady told her the price. *No, this is too expensive for me,* was Rose's first thought. She and her husband were saving their hard-earned money to buy furniture for their new small house in Bulgaria. The pink lady (she reminds Rose of the fairy godmother) again somehow sensed that getting this little doll was important to Rose. So, she took the delicate object from Rose's hands, skillfully wrapped it in the store's blue-and-white signature paper, and proudly said, "This is a present for you."

Rose shyly commented, "Oh, no, I could not possibly accept this expensive present!"

The saleslady started her quick chattering in German again. Rose was able to understand some of her explanation. The lady's daughter lives in another town and does not visit her mother often. Suddenly, Rose understood that giving this doll as a gift was just as important to the saleslady as it was important to Rose to get a first doll for her baby daughter. Rose said, "Danke" (Thank you) with deep appreciation.

"What is your name?" the pink lady asked her.

"Rose. And yours?"

"Gabriella," the lady answered with a vibrant laugh. The idea that this mature woman had a fashionable name made Rose laugh as well.

"Gabriella, what a beautiful name!" Rose told herself while she gave the lady a warm, appreciative handshake.

After Rose left the store, her body and soul felt warm from the coffee, and from the unexpected gift, which she had carefully placed inside the pocket of her winter coat. Rose hurried to get home. She should have taken the bus instead of walking. Now she was afraid that she would be late for work. Those Germans and their punctuality!

Later, Rose flew into her little apartment, where her husband was standing next to the window, most probably waiting for her return. He looked at his young bride curiously.

"Gabriella!" shouted Rose. Then she saw the puzzled look on her husband's face. "Gabriella will be our daughter's name."

❧ 2 ❧

Family Life in Germany

"In the world of bodies, we are all separate. In the world of spirit, we are all one."

– Marianne Williamson, "A Year of Daily Wisdom."

The big cafeteria that adjoins the chemical plant where Rose works was full at lunchtime. Rose hates the cigarette smoke, the smell of the food, and the hungry looks men give her when they look at her young, voluptuous body. Since she had put on some pounds during her pregnancy, Rose was walking at least one hour every day—regardless of the weather—and her body was getting strong. Her husband Miho Ivanov smiled warmly at her from the other side of the cafeteria. They both work the same shift, so she will not have to walk home alone, or take the bus home alone, after working at night.

The young family lives far away from the cafeteria, in a building with other Bulgarians and young people from various Eastern European countries. Rose liked the sense of community they have created with the other workers. It reminds her of the residents in the small village in Bulgaria she left long ago to get a better education and find better job prospects in the big city.

During the long, exhausting hours in the cafeteria, she allowed her mind to wander. Usually, her brain was flooded with images of the vast wheat fields of her country. Rose could vividly see their green color, speckled in Spring with the red color of poppy flowers. She could actually smell the roses and peonies in her mother's garden, and saw her mother working in the house, or in the big yard, smiling and singing. She could smell the tantalizing aroma of fresh home-baked banitsa—the famous Bulgarian pastry that is made with phyllo dough, feta cheese, and a mixture of eggs and yogurt.

Rose felt her husband's worried look upon her, so she smiled back at him with an expression that said, everything is fine. Her reassuring smile put him at ease. Rose loved to observe Miho from a distance. His tall, slender body, dark brown eyes and dark, almost black curly hair made him look distinguishably different from all the blond-haired, blue-eyed workers in the cafeteria. Their lunch shift would be over soon. The cafeteria workers usually ate their lunch after the plant workers were finished and their tables had been cleaned.

After lunch, Rose and her husband had the option to go home to rest in order to prepare for serving dinner at the cafeteria. Some days, they even visited the town with their fellow coworkers, enjoying a stroll along the streets, stopping at a bakery for a cup of coffee and a piece of German pastry. Today, however, few of their Bulgarian friends joined them.

The day was still sunny, but the cold afternoon breeze made them hurry to enter one of their favorite coffee shops.

Rose was anxious to share with her friends the name she and her husband had chosen for their little daughter. She wanted to tell them how well the baby was doing, flourishing slowly under the doctor's care. Maybe the worst experience was now behind them.

Her friends were excited to hear the news about her little beauty. "Gabriella—that is an unusual name," said Rose's friend Maria.

"Are you sure?"

"Yes, I am very sure," Rose answered with a smile. "And her nickname will be Gabby!" Gabriella's name meant "God is my strength," a truth the little girl would discover years later. At that time, ironically, neither Ivanov's family nor their friends believed in God. To them, the name sounded modern and German.

Rose explained to her friend the entire story about the saleslady in pink, and the little doll she received today from her, as a gift for her baby. Rose could not wait to go to her regular morning visit in the hospital to tell her story there.

Maria had a happy announcement to make on her own. She is expecting! All her friends cheered Maria and her husband, wishing they could celebrate such good news with alcohol, in the Bulgarian tradition. However, today was a working day; so the celebration had to wait for the weekend.

Rose and Maria were chatting about their future plans for their children, while their husbands were making plans for how to save money and buy themselves motorcycles. Little did they realize that this relationship they were developing now, in their 20s, would last throughout their lifetime.

The young Bulgarians had come to East Germany to work on a one-year contract. If the employer—the big chemical plant in the town of Schwedt in northeastern Brandenburg state, on the border with Poland, was satisfied by their work, they could extend their contract with an additional year. This opportunity, however, was not available to many of their peers in Bulgaria. At that time, it was difficult to leave one's homeland, even to work in another Socialist country.

Since the Communist Party of Bulgaria did not allow citizens to travel freely, young Bulgarians did not want to lose this once-in-a-lifetime opportunity to improve their circumstances. Both the women's families were anxious about how Maria's pregnancy and Gabriella's health would affect their plans to live in Germany for one more year. Rose will have to stop working and take maternity leave when Gabby is discharged from the hospital. Although the future was unknown, Maria and Rose were hopeful, with that typical blissful ignorance people often have during their young adult life.

After the dinner shift was over, Rose and her husband Miho rode the bus to their apartment building on the other side of town. Later that night, lying in bed in the dark and hugging, he buried his head in her long, fragrant hair. "Do you think she is improving?" Their little girl was always on their minds.

"It seems like she is. I am nursing her when I can, and the doctors and nurses take good care of her. Maybe we will be able to take her home in a few months." Rose then fell asleep peacefully in her husband's arms.

3

A Visit to the Hospital

"Miracles occur naturally as expressions of love."

– Marianne Williamson, "A Year of Daily Wisdom."

When Rose and Miho woke up the next morning, the bedroom windows were thick with ice from the cold wind and the new snowfall. Winters in this northern country were harsh. Rose was anxious about how she would get to the hospital today; the couple had an agreement that she would go almost every morning to see their daughter.

Miho usually woke up later in the morning. So, sometimes they went to the hospital together in the afternoon, after their lunch shift. Rose liked it better when her husband accompanied her when visiting their baby. Today, he was awake early and wanted to travel there with her. "No walking today," he smiled gently. They had a quick breakfast of boiled eggs, the spicy sausage Weisswurst (whitish German sausage made chiefly of veal), and a cup of coffee. In Germany, not only the coffee became a favorite drink for Rose; this sausage also became a favorite breakfast food for them both. After that, they hurried, yet walked carefully, to catch the bus that would take them directly to the hospital. Rose held her husband's arm firmly. She could feel his strong muscles under his thick, dark winter coat. The streets were covered with soft snow that looked like cotton, but underneath some spots, treacherously, there was ice hidden under the snow.

The bus was comfortably warm and clean, another striking difference between buses in Germany and the dilapidated ones in Bulgaria. Rose was anxious to get to the hospital so she could see how her daughter was doing. They were greeted with warm smiles by the nurses and the young doctor. By now, everyone there knew Rose and Miho, and the hospital's premature baby wing had started to feel like a second home to them. The young doctor Altman, whose last name was not appropriate at all (the meaning was an old man) took the parents aside. "She is a fighter, your tiny girl," he said with passion. They learned that Gabriella had eaten and slept well last night.

Rose told the doctor that they had chosen the name Gabriella. The hospital personnel were pleased that the name was of German origin. The irony was, however, that the name actually had a Jewish origin, which Gabby would learn later in her life. Rose asked the doctor if she could put the little porcelain doll next to her baby. Since the doctor had some concerns about the doll transmitting infections, one of the nurses suggested putting the doll outside the incubator and promised that everyone would be careful not to break her. Rose seemed satisfied by this turn of events.

Miho asked the doctor, with concern, when they would be able to take their daughter home. The answer was, if she keeps improving at the current speed, probably in mid-April. This wonderful news made the faces of the young couple glow; they smiled at each other.

The parents spent one hour with their little girl. Both were convinced that she was smiling at them, even though the nurses were trying to explain that it was too early for her to be able to make a real smile. They were also told that Gabriella might reach her milestones later than other children. Nevertheless, the young couple was convinced that their daughter was unique and she would eventually outshine her peers. In Bulgaria, there is a popular saying that parents and grandparents use to praise their children or grandchildren: "Our little bird is the most beautiful and smart."

Ivanov's family decided to call their parents in Bulgaria to share the good news about the baby. They usually communicate with their homeland through calls placed by a lady who works at the Central post station in the town in Germany. On the other receiving end was the post office in the little village in Bulgaria where Rose's parents live. However, there was only one phone at the local post station. Rose usually calls and speaks with the post office clerk, the post woman there, who then tries to find Rose's mother at the middle school where she works.

After waiting about 20 minutes, Rose called again and was able to speak with her mother, Iona. Rose shared with her the happy news about her baby.

Her mother, however, was not that pleased to learn about the chosen name for the girl, Gabriella. In fact, the grandmothers on both sides were hoping that the baby would be named after one of them. This, after all, was an ancient Bulgarian tradition.

At the same time, Iona was very happy that her granddaughter's health was improving and that she would be going home soon with her parents. When would the family be coming home to Bulgaria? That was the question her mother asked every single time they talked on the phone.

Rose tried a few times to write letters to her parents and her parents-in-law. But the postal service was so unreliable; sometimes the letters were received over a month after they were sent. So, she finally gave up on writing letters and now she called her family once every two weeks.

Now it was Miho's turn to call his parents, who live in a neighborhood close to Varna, a big city on the Black Sea. His parents were one of the first families in the neighborhood to get a home phone, a luxury unheard-of at that time. So now some of their neighbors would come to his parents' house when they wanted to place phone calls.

Miho's mother answered right away; she was probably waiting next to the phone. It had been two weeks since his last call, and his mother was hoping they would call soon. She, as well, made it clear that she was not pleased by the baby's chosen name, and she asked the same questions as Iona: When are they coming home? When are they bringing their first granddaughter home from the hospital? Half-satisfied by her son's answers, Dona, Miho's mother, finally shared with him that his father was not feeling well. He probably will be placed in the hospital soon for observation.

When the conversation ended, Miho shared the news with his wife. Maybe it was time to go home soon. Their parents needed them, and they needed their parents' help to raise Gabby.

4

Rose's Sweet Memories

*"When our minds are filled with light,
there is no room for darkness."*

– Marianne Williamson "A Year of Daily Wisdom."

Spring came early this year. The days became longer and warmer. Rose was taking her customary morning walk with Gabby, who was sleeping peacefully in her pink stroller. Rose quickly crossed the busy Berliner Strasse (one of the main streets in the town) and entered the beautiful waterfront park that followed along the River Oder. Most of the almond trees in the park were blooming. She enjoyed looking at their white and pink blossoms. From a distance, they looked like brides dressed in gorgeous gowns. Rose smiled at that image of brides. She remembered her big, traditional Bulgarian wedding. After all, it was just held last summer.

Rose sat at one of the benches at the park under a blooming almond tree. The sun was shining brightly; birds were everywhere, singing beautifully. Rose was deeply engrossed in memories of her wedding day, which was sunny and bright, like today. That wedding morning, she saw herself through the eyes of her loving husband-to-be.

Miho was waiting for his bride-to-be to get into the car. She appeared calm and very elegant in her tea-length white lace dress. Her long, brown hair was pinned up, and her white bridal veil made her look like a princess. Her makeup was very light and had been tastefully done by her best friend, Maria. Miho kissed Rose's lips and all the guests cheered "Gorchivo!" which means "The wine is bitter, so sweeten it by kissing each other." Rose smiled. This was their first official kiss, in front of all their guests and their parents.

Gabby started to wiggle about in the stroller, disrupting her mother's sweet memories. Rose looked at her wristwatch; it was time to feed her baby. Rose had tried hard to nurse her daughter in the hospital whenever she could. Due to the irregular nursing schedule, her milk production had ceased. Now she was giving her the newest invention—a baby formula. Gabby seemed to like it. The little girl's weight was steadily improving; she was growing, but still looked small for her age.

After she was fed, Gabby fell asleep again. The doctors insisted that she have a strict feeding and sleeping schedule. Rose was determined to follow their medical advice strictly, since she wanted her daughter to grow up healthily.

Rose tried to read the book she had brought with her to the park. But she had not realized that the book had slipped away from her hands onto the ground. Her mind rapidly went back to the events of last summer.

Before Rose and Miho took their work assignment and left for Germany, they decided to get married. This was supposed to make life easier for them, to be a family living in a foreign country. They could get a bigger apartment and perhaps shorter shifts. A couple who was supposed to travel to Germany with them were also getting married. So, after their short courtship and an engagement that lasted only a few months, Rose and Miho set a wedding date in mid-summer.

Their parents were stressed by the huge task of organizing a wedding in such a short time. After all, most of the relatives on both sides, and many friends, have to be invited to such an important family event. In fact, they were expecting around 200 guests. Planning a wedding was made even more difficult by the constant shortage of all kinds of goods in Bulgarian stores at that time.

One of the most difficult issues appeared to be finding the right fabric for the wedding gown. After spending hours of her free time searching for the right material, Rose was ready to give up. One sunny day, she was strolling through the city commercial district, when she met an old girlfriend, Katya. They got ice cream at the closest pastry shop and sat inside to catch up with each other's news. Rose was sad to learn about her friend's recent broken engagement. She was debating whether to tell her or not about her own upcoming wedding. After all, this was her close girlfriend she had known since childhood.

Finally, Rose shared with Katya her good news about her own wedding. She also shared her disappointment about not being able to find the right fabric for her wedding gown. Just then, her girlfriend offered to give Rose a piece of the white lace fabric that had been bought for her own wedding gown from France. Rose was both thrilled and sad. Her childhood friend had indeed given her a priceless gift.

Now every time Rose looked at her black-and-white wedding photographs, she thought about her friend. She would certainly tell this bittersweet story to her daughter when she grows up.

A few weeks after they got married, the newlyweds left their country to take their assignment in Germany. This was the first flight for each of them, and also their first flight together as a couple. Rose was anxious and a little worried when she was seated in the airplane. Her husband's calm behavior put her at ease. She took a place next to a window and was enjoying the view. Miho was drinking his coffee and smoking. His young bride could not take her eyes off him.

She remembered when the two had first met at the vocational school for bartenders and waiters. His dark, strong features were quite striking, and, along with his calm behavior, attracted her to him instantly. He was different from other men at the school, who still looked and behaved like teenagers. Her future husband was mature well beyond his age. She was truly surprised to learn that he was older than she by only two years.

She fell in love with him right away. Shortly after that meeting, they started dating. And here they are now, newly married, on an airplane that will take them to a new adventure in a foreign country.

❦ 5 ❦

Traveling Back Home to Bulgaria

"The search for inner peace is a lifestyle decision."

– Marianne Williamson, "A Year of Daily Wisdom."

Rose's second flight was not as happy as her first one. But her young, optimistic nature made her not dwell long on the circumstances. Miho was hugging her tightly at Berlin's airport. She was flying back home with tiny Gabby. Miho was staying behind to finish his one-year work contract, hoping to secure one more additional year; they needed the money. The young father kissed his baby daughter gently and his wife passionately. He waved goodbye to them at the gate.

Rose was seated again next to the window on the airplane, as she had been on the previous flight. She had one of the front seats this time, so the baby could be placed inside the safety harness. Surprisingly for Rose, Gabby was tolerating the trip quite well. The little Tinker, who was 4 months old now, smiled charmingly at the flight attendant. Rose was impressed by the flight crew. Probably the same age as she was, they were doing everything possible to make her and her daughter comfortable.

Gabby was taking a nap now, while Rose rested her head on the window frame. She could only see white clouds and sun rays. Soon she and her baby would be returning home, after a long time abroad. She left as a young bride and is returning now as a young mother.

What is waiting for her in the near future? Since her husband is in Germany, she decided to live at her parents' house in the village while she waits for his return. It will be very helpful to have her mother and her younger sister around, and it will be better for her daughter to grow up outside a big city. In the village, the air is not polluted; the food comes not from stores, but from her grandparents' land and farm. Gabby would have more space to run and play there when she gets older. Rose was thinking about starting to look at the possibilities for furthering her own education. If she enrolls at the local college in the fall, she will definitely need her parents' help.

Her parents-in-law greeted Rose at the airport upon her arrival, and were enthralled to finally meet their granddaughter. "She is so small!" her mother-in-law said.

"But she is healthy," Rose answered firmly. Rose sensed that her parents-in-law, Dona and Ivan, were not happy about their daughter-in-law's decision to go back to her parents. Miho's parents would much rather have Rose and the baby live at the new house they had built as a wedding gift for the young family.

But Rose had chosen to go back to her parents' old house in the village. How disappointing! How would Dona and Ivan answer their neighbors' and relatives' questions? Public opinion was important to them. Although nothing was said about the decision, the air in the car was heavy with disapproval.

Despite their disappointment, Miho's parents drove Rose and Gabby to the village. Ivan drove skillfully. He was very proud of his newly acquired car; Since the auto industry was government-controlled, many people waited years to get a car. So traffic was light, especially outside the big cities.

The trip did not take long. Rose's heart started beating fast when she saw the familiar entrance to her birthplace. Massive poplar trees stood on both sides of the road, forming a lush green canopy that made the entrance look surreal, almost like an enchanted forest. She glanced at the black-and-white sign of the village's name, "Krasen," which means "beautiful" in Bulgarian. Indeed, to Rose, this *was* the most beautiful place on Earth.

Rose's parents greeted everyone with a smile and a hug. Iona, who had tears of joy in her eyes, was overjoyed to see her daughter and granddaughter. Dimo, Rose's father, usually did not show much emotion. He hugged his daughter and took his granddaughter into his hands. Gabby immediately decided that this was the most comfortable place for her—resting in her grandfather's arms. The baby kept smiling at him and cooing. It was clear that the lifelong bond between the two had been made at that very moment.

A big feast with an abundance of food and drinks in a typical Bulgarian style had been prepared by Rose's parents. Many friends, relatives and neighbors from the village had been invited. Everyone wanted to see the baby girl who had been born abroad. The crowded table sat under the shadows of the fruit trees in the big yard. People were already having a good time. Even Rose's parents-in-law were able to put their worries aside for a while and enjoy the feast.

Rose was feeling so happy on this festive day, surrounded by her relatives and her childhood friends. Although she would have some days when she succumbed to wistful thoughts about her husband being away for more months, Rose would wait patiently for Miho's return, and in the meantime, she would devote all her energy to her daughter and her studies.

⚬ **6** ⚬

Aunt Ani

"An aunt is a double blessing.
She loves like a parent, and acts like a friend."

– Author Unknown

On this cold November morning, Gabby woke her grandmother up early. The girl had gotten used to her strict schedule of feeding, playing and sleeping. She was about 10 months old now, and fun to be around. Since early morning, the small house was filled with her happy chattering and laughing. She was able to say a few distinguishable words, like "ta-ta" and "ba-ba" (grandmother in Bulgarian). Iona's favorite game with Gabby was to organize all the toys in the crib and ask her, "Where is the dog, the bear, the doll?" Gabby chose the correct toy each time. In her grandparents' and her aunt's adoring eyes, Gabby was the most beautiful, unique, and smart baby. Gabby especially liked the little red-white-and-blue porcelain doll. Each time they showed her the doll, she said "ma-ma."

Could the baby associate the little doll with her missing mother, Iona wondered? After all, Rose had left the village a few months ago to go back to live in the big city. She and Miho, who had returned from his assignment in Germany by that time, were both enrolled at the College of Tourism, and came to visit their daughter when possible.

Iona was in a hurry to get to work. She woke up her younger daughter, Ani. The young woman recently graduated from high school and had decided to postpone her further studies, as she was helping her parents with the housework. She also was taking care of the baby during week-days, since both of her parents had jobs. Ani adored her little niece. Later in life, she always joked that Gabby was her first daughter.

There was not much to do during winter months in the village. Gabby's grandparents did not own a television set, which was a luxury unheard-of at that time. The old radio in the house was on all day long, as Gabby seemed to like listening to any type of music. Ani was wondering where to take Gabby for a walk after she had fed and changed her. Except for the library, the post office, one mom-and-pop store that sells everything imaginable, and a small pastry shop, there was nowhere to go. The town also had a small movie theater, open only on weekends.

The day was sunny, but bitterly cold. After she dressed the baby warmly, Ani put her in the pink stroller and they took a short walk to the village school, where Iona was working. The building was heated, and full of life. Gabby liked the happy chatter coming from the students. All the teachers and staff adored the baby. Ani usually spent a few hours with her at the school, or at the local library. When Gabby was sleeping, Ani could read and study.

At noontime, Ani got the baby's food for that day from the local children's kitchen, a very convenient service for young mothers since then they did not have to cook each day separately for their babies and husbands. The kitchen provided nutritious warm food every day of the working week. Plus, local young parents could meet there, exchange news and chat about the latest books.

Ani could not wait for spring to come, so she could take long walks with Gabby around the village, the little nearby forest and the wheat fields. Sometimes the teachers from the local kindergarten allowed Ani and Gabby to participate in their field trips. It was too early to actually put Gabby in the first group of kindergarten, however, which usually takes kids who are 3 years old. In the big cities, there are "yaslas"—between daycare and pre-kindergarten. Usually, parents left their young toddlers in a yasla on Mondays and picked them up on Fridays. This idea did not sound appealing to Gabby's parents, nor to her grandparents and her aunt. Plus, Gabby was too young for the yasla. So, Ani devoted her time and energy raising the little girl for a few years until Rose graduates from college. Gabby truly became first of Ani's children.

7

The Twin Sisters Were Born

"My siblings are my best friends"

– "An Intrinsic Coach," by Hugh Warren, an American
producer and a writer about personal development.

Gabby was lying comfortably on Rose's pregnant belly, singing a song. A few minutes before that, the 3-year-old girl was playing with her "doctor's instrument"—a toy stethoscope—to listen to the "sounds" the baby was making. Since Rose had explained to Gabby that she could listen to baby's heartbeat, the little girl played this fascinating game a few times a day. Rose was almost nine months pregnant; she and Miho had been preparing Gabby for her new role of big sister for a while. From books, games and explanations, the little girl got used to the idea that she was going to share her Mom, Dad and toys with her new little brother.

Rose remembered one recent visit to the store when Gabby had asked for a toy. Rose told her that they were saving money for the new baby. Gabby's disappointed face was worth capturing in the picture. Later the same day, still remembering her earlier disappointment, the little girl said, "I am not going to share my dolls with my brother. He needs to get his own toys!"

Rose stroked her daughter's head absent-mindedly. This second pregnancy was much more difficult than the first. Even with the scare of giving birth at only 6 months of gestation when she was pregnant with Gabby, Rose was glowing and handling the changes of pregnancy easily then. This time, her face was covered with brown spots; she had gained lots of weight, so it was difficult for her to walk, and her ankles were often swollen. She needed to rest more often and had to stop working earlier. Rose was grateful that the pregnancy was not during the winter, so she did not need to put on heavy winter shoes or boots.

A few days later, Gabby woke up one morning and started looking for Rose. She found her Aunt Ani in the kitchen, preparing breakfast. "Where is my Mommy?" the little girl asked.

Her aunt smiled secretively and replied, "You are a big sister now, Gabby! You have *two* little sisters!" Ani saw the puzzled look on her niece's face and was not sure how to handle the situation. She decided to leave the rest of the explanation about the twins to Gabby's parents.

After Gabby was fed and dressed, she, her aunt and her father went to visit Rose and the twin sisters in the hospital. Gabby always enjoyed riding in her grandfather's car; Miho had borrowed his Dad's car for the occasion. Gabby's face was glued to the car's window. She was excited to observe the passing buildings and people and counted them.

The big hospital looked scary to her. "Are there that many babies in this building?!" Gabby asked. She walked quickly, holding her father's hand tightly. At that time, visitations were usually prohibited in most of the Bulgarian hospitals due to the risk of hospital-acquired infections. This new, modern hospital was the first one to implement such an innovative idea as open visiting policy.

Rose was alone in the room with the twin girls, another new innovation. Usually, two or three women occupied one room in the maternity ward; their babies were kept in the nursery and were brought to the mothers' room only during feeding times. Rose was happy to keep her new daughters close to her. Still, even with all the progress, this hospital was far behind the times compared to the one in Germany where Gabby was born.

Gabby gave her Mom a quick kiss, curiously looking at the babies. "Why are they two brothers?" she asked, as Rose and Miho smiled patiently at her. After a few minutes of explanation, Gabby realized that in fact the babies were girls. "Can you please return them and get my little brother?" she insisted. Her mother answered that babies are not toys, and that parents cannot return them. "Well, keep them, then," Gabby pouted. "But I am going back to my grandparents' house in the village, and I am taking all my toys with me." After Gabby threw this tantrum, Rose realized that her little girl might be correct. They would need the help of her parents again to raise Gabby. With the twins in the house, and Miho working different shifts, Rose's hands would be very full.

It was as much a surprise for Ivanov's family that Rose had delivered two girls on one warm September day. All the new clothes and bedding were blue, to greet the expected boy! At that time, ultrasound was not available to determine the number or gender of the fetuses. Somehow, the doctors and midwives had missed the sound of two heartbeats. The twin girls were named after both of their grandmothers—Dona and Iona. The ancient Bulgarian tradition finally had been followed! This made the grandmothers incredibly happy and proud that their names would be preserved for the next generation, and eventually to eternity, if the girls' granddaughters would be named after their grandmothers as well.

Gabby was so happy to get back to Iona and Dimo's house. This time she was enrolled in the local kindergarten. Gabby had one of the best childhoods possible! She was doted on and spoiled by her grandparents. During the cold winter mornings, Dimo brought a basin of warm water to her bed for his granddaughter to wash her face. After that, he played horsy while dragging the sleigh, with Gabby warmly dressed inside it, through the snow on the way to the kindergarten. Gabby sang all the way to school. And every day Iona cooked wholesome, healthy meals for her granddaughter.

At night Iona put Gabby to sleep and told her made-up fairytales and bedtime stories. Gabby remembered to this day the scary folklore tale about the Torbalan—the mythical villain who carries a torba (a sack) on his back. Parents and grandparents to this day frighten their children and grandchildren with the tale when they misbehave. Gabby was worried that Torbalan would come to kidnap her and carry her somewhere far away from her home.

Gabby made lots of lifelong friendships among the local children. Kids at that time were free to explore the village on their own during weekends and vacations and played on the streets and at the local park from dusk until dawn.

Despite the selfless devotion of her grandparents and all the friendships she built in the village, Gabby always felt she was missing something. She needed her mother, her father and her little sisters in her life. Especially on March 8, Mother's Day, when other children were giving presents and flowers to their mothers, the girl's heart was full of sorrow. Although Rose visited her little daughter in the village as much as possible, she also brought the twins, so Gabby was able to develop a good bond with her siblings.

Finally, Rose and Miho made the decision that their daughter would start school in the city, not in the village. Gabby was happy that she would be living with her parents and sisters at last. But at the same time, she did not want to leave her grandparents and her village friends. Was life often going to put her in situations when she would not be happy with either the choices she had made or the ones that were made for her?

PART II

❧ **1** ❧

Gabby is Starting Elementary School

"Today is the first day of the rest of your life"

– Attributed to Charles E. "Chuck" Dederich, Sr., (1913-
1997), founder of Synanon, a self-help community in
California for drug abusers and alcoholics.

It was a warm and sunny day, September 15, the traditional first day of the school year in Bulgaria. The schoolyard was full of children of all ages, dressed in their best clothes. Most of the students were holding big bouquets of flowers for the teachers. Both parents and teachers were enjoying the feeling of a holiday that would soon disappear into everyday mundane tasks. The yard resonated with the silvery laughter of the happy kids. The first-graders were organized on the front row of all classes in the yard. They all seemed excited and scared at the same time. Gabby was one of them. With her new yellow school backpack, she was thrilled to enter the school building.

She had seen a school full of children before, of course. In her grandparents' village, her aunt Iona brought Gabby with her to school almost every day. Some of the teachers even allowed her to attend their classes. One of her favorite classrooms was geography, with all the maps and the globe of the world. Gabby dreamt of traveling the world. She also enjoyed the music room, full of different instruments, and loved to attend biology classes as well. She looked with fearless curiosity at the big jars filled with yellow liquid and animal parts. She was not scared at all.

But her favorite room in the school was the linguistic teaching studio. In that class, students with headphones were isolated in individual wooden booths with a single window. The teacher worked at a platform that looked like a command center with colored buttons. This was fascinating to Gabby. She could stay in this room for hours, listening to students repeating sentences in different languages. After spending most of her early childhood in school, Gabby was, of course, dreaming of becoming a teacher.

So, in her first real day at school as a first-grader, she was not a bit scared. Yes, this school might have been bigger and louder than the village school, but children were the same everywhere. Gabby looked at her classmates with curiosity, and quickly made friends with the ease that only young children can. Her heart was kind; she was open and polite to children and teachers alike.

To this day, Gabby remembers the first time she said her full name when the teacher asked each child in the classroom their name. Gabriella Mihova Ivanova, she answered in her lilting voice, smiling at the young woman who would become as important to her as her own mother for the next few years of her elementary education.

School was easy for Gabby. She had known how to read and write since she was four years old; her grandmother taught her well. The girl was enrolled at one of the best, most elite schools in town. Since first grade, education was taught in both Russian and Bulgarian languages. Later on, Gabriella would start studying English as well.

From her early school years, Gabby remembered mostly the games she played with her classmates, on the school playground before and after school and in-between periods. In the winter, kids made their own winter slides using recycled wood or plastic material, and played outside until it was dark and time to go home and study.

Gabby and one of her best friends in school, Vera, invented lots of mischievous games and situations, such as hiding in the secret places at school in order to miss classes. On another occasion, Vera and Gabby went after school to the outskirts of town to take some grapes from the local vineyard. That late afternoon, they put their parents under tremendous stress, since they thought the two girls got lost. The situation was eventually resolved when the girls came back safely to their homes. Needless to say, they each were grounded for a while.

Of course, they could not beat the boys at the school, who were involved in all types of havoc, such as breaking windows with a ball while playing soccer; skipping school to go to the movies, and hiding live frogs in the classroom in order to disrupt the study process. That was the way children figured out how to be social, practical, to learn from their mistakes, and to appreciate the similarities and differences between people.

Gabby and Vera shared their little secrets with each other. They talked about the boys they thought were attractive. "Oh, that blond-haired boy who is one year older than us; I like him!" Gabby said one day.

"Me, too…" Vera answered.

"But he fought with me first!" Gabby cried out.

"Well, then I will fight with the brown-haired boy I like," Vera responded.

Problems get solved so easily when you are children. Soon, they were playing together again at the school playground. "Vera, do you want to play with my porcelain doll? But please be careful because she is fragile. I will tell you the story of this doll. My Mom found it in a magical store in Germany when I was just a little baby." Vera would listen to this story with rapt attention for many years to come.

Children at that time were much more independent than children today. Gabby took the city bus to school when she was just seven years old. She walked by herself to the grocery store, or the library. She went to the movies with her friends or classmates, without chaperones. During the warm summer days, children would play on the streets until midnight, and no parent or grandparent was concerned about their whereabouts—even if they had not seen them all day. They knew that their children eventually would come home when they got hungry, or sleepy.

Most of Gabby's summer vacations were spent in the village. She was happy to play with her old friends from kindergarten. Her sisters and her cousins, Ani's children, often spent the summer at the village as well. Children from all ages played together, inventing interesting games, riding bikes all day long, rummaging through the local gardens for fruits.

Gabby even organized local kids in groups, like girl scout/ boy scout groups. They played ball, spies, and hide-and-seek at the local park. The summer was their special time, spent mostly outdoors. During the cooler summer afternoons, children went to the local movie theater, and, afterwards, enjoyed ice cream from the local pastry shop. They had no concerns about the future. Adulthood seemed far away and bright.

Gabby read lots of books during her vacation. Every school at that time provided a list of recommended books that students were supposed to finish reading during vacation. When she was not playing outside, Gabby was lying in her bed, in the comfort of the cool house, reading. *"Maybe I should reconsider my dream of becoming a teacher. I am going to be a writer!"* Gabby thought to herself.

❧ **2** ❧

Teenage Gabby Learns Things About Boys

"Love goes toward love, as school-boys from their books,
But love from love, toward school with heavy looks."

– William Shakespeare, "Romeo and Juliet" 1597, Act II,
Scene 2, line 156

Gabby was waiting at the bus station. Public buses at that time were usually late. She had plenty of time to think about this boy from school. He was two years older than she, and had blue eyes and blond hair. When she talked to him today, her heart was pounding, and the palms of her hands were wet. He seemed to be oblivious to her feelings.

On the other hand, Gabby's sensitive, romantic nature made her fall in love effortlessly. She was an easily impressed girl. Most of the time, she lived inside the world of whatever book she was reading. There was nothing sexual or erotic in her mind about this boy. She had not even allowed herself to dream about their first kiss. Her fantasies about him varied, depending on her mood and the day. Most often she imagined going to a movie with him or eating ice cream together. Other times her dreams went wild. She allowed herself to imagine being married to him and having children together.

Gabby was entertained by her fantasies. In her mind, she had built a perfect life with this boy. Today, while waiting at the bus station, she was dreaming of the house they would be living in. She saw each detail vividly—down to the furniture and to the color of the curtains they would choose together. Gabby had read that people who dream frequently become good storytellers and writers.

Of course, she was not sharing her fantasies with her friends, or her parents. When she was younger, she kept a diary. One day, her cousin had discovered that notebook with all her secrets inside; he teased her constantly about them. So, Gabby made a promise to keep her thoughts and dreams to herself in the future.

Her girlfriend Vera knew that Gabby was interested in this particular boy; Vera had her own heartaches. The two teenage girls met at the park on this sunny spring day. They were supposed to be studying for the upcoming exams, but instead, they planned to take a long walk at the Seaside garden and share their thoughts and experiences with boys. Both girls were good students, but as they reached adolescent years, their earlier childhood mischievousness had devolved toward discussing boys. Vera started dating her longtime admirer in secrecy from her parents, and Gabby had to hear all the details about her first date.

The friends were walking slowly along the heavenly-looking aisles of the garden, holding hands and talking. They were enjoying spring in full bloom and the love songs of the birds. While talking and laughing, they suddenly realized they had reached the small "bridge of the wishes." Most of the children, teenagers, and even some adults, believed that if you pass the bridge walking backwards, your wishes would be fulfilled. Gabby and Vera laughingly crossed the bridge in the proper way. To be sure their wishes would become true, they even closed their eyes while walking backwards. *"Please, let me see this boy soon,"* Gabby wished.

On their way back to Vera's home, the girls unexpectedly saw a group of boys riding their bikes. Gabby's young love was among them. The girl's heart started to race; the boy looked at her impishly while passing by. Gabby smiled back at him. The sun started shining brighter; the birds' songs seemed more charming than ever. He paid attention to her after all! She then understood that their attraction was mutual.

At Vera's place, the girls ate a hearty lunch and finally got to their studies. Next day, they had to take their exams. Soon, the school year would be over.

Along with the rest of their classmates, they will spend some of the summer months in a village not far from town. All school-aged children were required to spend at least one month on agricultural work. They picked fruits or vegetables and lived in camps. It was a good motivator for children to spend time working in the fresh air. Of course, at that time, neither the children nor their parents appreciated it when they were taken away from their families during summer vacation. It did seem like taking advantage of child labor. However, in the long run, this endeavor taught children how to work at hard jobs and how to work on a team, how to live in close quarters, and how to build strong friendships. In other words, it prepared them for hardships that might arise in their future lives.

Gabby and Vera would have many more school years together that were filled with devotion to their studies; many interesting school trips; young loves, heartbreaks and disappointments. Their relationship would, however, withstand the passage of time, as well as separations.

3

Gabby Meets Aaron

During her senior year of high school, Gabby was scheduling her time between school, taking private lessons to get into a prestigious college, and working at the local library. She grew up to be a smart and good-looking young woman. Despite her difficulty coming into this world, now she was healthy, and her body was petite but strong. She inherited both the deep, dark brown eyes of her father and his dark brown, wavy hair. From her mother she got her pale white skin color, her elegance and her grace. Her demeanor was sunny, and she was ready to laugh at any time.

Gabby was working at the local library, located in an old building with high ceilings, that day. She usually arrived at work after finishing school for the day and having her lunch at the school cafeteria. She spent a few hours at the library before she went home to study. Some Sundays, she worked all day.

Today, Gabby was climbing a ladder to reach some books on the top of the high cabinet.

She saw a young man walking toward her. He had a dark olive complexion, in striking contrast to his intelligent deep-green eyes. To complete the impression of perfection, his face was encircled with a cloud of curly dark brown hair. The young man smiled at her. "Do you need any help, young lady?" His white teeth were sparkling when he smiled.

Gabby thought, *"This is one of the handsomest men I have ever set eyes on."*

By this age, she already knew how to handle the increased heartbeats and sweaty palms that surfaced when she met an impressive male. She gracefully got down from the ladder. "No, I do not need any help. But thank you for offering." The young man took her hand and tenderly kissed it with the ease of a gentleman; Gabby was utterly surprised by this gesture. This classy behavior was uncommon in a Communist country where people address each other as "comrades" and shake hands when meeting. Her eyes widened, and for a few seconds, she was not able to control her racing heartbeat.

"Aaron," the young man introduced himself.

"Gabriella," she answered. Gabby quickly recovered from her uneasiness and assumed her professional demeanor.

The man was looking for some medical titles. "The books you want can be found up on the second floor, on the left. One of the titles, however, would need to be ordered. Are you a medical student?" the young woman asked boldly.

"I will answer your question only if you agree to have coffee with me," Aaron responded with a mischievous smile.

Gabby had heard this proposal before and she usually answered "no." This time, she felt defenseless against the charm of this good-looking man and said, "I am working until six."

"I will be waiting for you at the door when you finish," Aaron smiled charmingly.

"What am I getting myself into?" Gabby asked herself after Aaron went off to the second floor. Precisely at six o'clock, the young man was waiting for her at the front door of the library. He offered to take her to one of the local pastry shops, which happened to be a favorite of Gabby's. She decided not to share this information with him, and not to reveal a lot about herself in general during this first date.

"Aaron is not a Bulgarian name, is it?" Gabby asked a question first.

"No. It is a Jewish name," he answered.

"You are Jewish?" Whether this was a question or a statement from Gabby was not clear.

"Yes, I am," Aaron said, looking her straight in the eyes. His gaze made her knees weak—thank God she was sitting down! She quietly ate her pastry and drank her cup of *bosa*—the famous Bulgarian fermented drink made from barley. It was late for a coffee. "Gabriella is not a typical Bulgarian name, either" Aaron observed half-jokingly.

Gabby smiled at him in return. "I was born in Germany." *Am I revealing too much already?*

The two were curious about each other, but neither wanted to divulge too much too fast. Gabby felt as if she was observing herself from a distance. This was a strange feeling, almost like an out-of-body experience. Why is she so attracted to this man? She just met him a few hours ago. Usually, she likes men with blond hair. He is older than she, and his behavior and gentlemanly manners are uncommon. Gabby had limited experience with boys, mostly of her own age. This man was confusing to her, and she did not know how to behave, or what to expect from him. Nothing she had read in books about men could guide her in this situation.

Aaron was also closely observing the young woman. He sensed that she was confused and scared, so he touched her hand to calm her down. This friendly gesture had the opposite effect on Gabby. The place where he had touched her delicate little hand was burning now; her heart was absolutely racing. She hoped that her face was not red from blushing, thereby giving away her emotions.

Aaron started to talk about his studies and his plans, hoping this would calm her down. Gabby was listening to his deep, smooth, melodic voice—the voice of a singer. "Are you a musician?" She was surprised by her own question.

"I do play a guitar sometimes, yes. Do you want to hear me play and sing? I can take you to my apartment right now and show you my guitar..." He smirked with a devilish smile. Gabby raised her arched eyebrows in pure astonishment. *He is surely bold, this man*, she thought to herself.

Aaron offered to walk Gabby to the bus station, and she accepted gratefully. After all, it was dark outside, and the streets were almost empty. The two young people were walking slowly, close to each other, not touching, just smiling and talking. Suddenly, both were overcome by the knowledge that they would have to separate soon. The young man stopped walking and leaned toward Gabby, held her waist gently and kissed her. *His lips were soft, and his breath smelled like strawberry wine*, Gabby thought. His kiss was gentle, but passionate. She had never been kissed in such a way before. She felt dizzy and light-headed at the same time—as if she was drunk with that same strawberry wine.

Gabby did not know how to kiss well. She had experienced a few stolen kisses before, from two boys from her school. But she had almost felt nothing then. This kiss was different. This kiss had shaken her to her core. She responded passionately—much to her own surprise. She did not want their lips to separate. She wanted this moment to last as long as possible. She wanted to touch his face, his body. She felt like an insect caught in a spider web. She could not escape even if she wanted to; but she did not want to.

Gabby did not remember how she got home. Had she taken the bus? They must have said goodbye to each other. Suddenly, she froze as she entered her house. She and Aaron had not exchanged phone numbers. *"How is he ever going to be able to find me again?!"*

⟨ **4** ⟩

Love Turns Out to Be a Difficult Task

"Your task is not to seek for love, but merely to seek and find all the barriers within yourself that you have built against it."

– Rumi (1207–1273). Rumi was a 13th century Persian poet, theologian, Sufi mystic and scholar. His influence transcends national borders and ethnic divisions.

Gabby's mind was wandering. Any time she closed her eyes, she saw Aaron's face. She could still feel his soft, warm lips on hers. Her body was burning to be near his. She was hugging her pillow, imagining she was hugging her newfound lover's strong, masculine body.

No, she did not have time for love right now. She has plans: her studies, her job, and her schooling. She is graduating next year from high school. Her plan after graduation is to study to be a journalist in the capital of Bulgaria. Aaron seems to be devoted to his studies as well. So, really, they do not have time

51

for a relationship. At the same time, she unconsciously sensed that something unusual and significant had just happened in her life. Whatever it was filled her heart with happiness and hope.

"But how will he find me, since I am not working tomorrow?" Gabby's thoughts were suddenly racing. She made a pact with herself—if he finds her, somehow, in the next couple of days, she will go out with him again (if he asks her, of course). But what if he already has a girlfriend, or a wife? The young woman's heart sank. No, that cannot be, as he said he is only five years older than she. She did not see a wedding band on Aaron's ring finger. But…maybe Jewish people do not wear wedding bands.

Gabby was a very intelligent and smart young woman. Despite that, somehow, she was naïve about men. Her classmates were so easy for her to read. But regarding this man, she did not know what to expect, or how to read him. He was very polite, yet very assertive, and her sensitive soul detected quickly that he was hiding some secrets. He seemed conflicted. She did not know what the conflict was, but she would find out.

It was time to go to sleep; tomorrow was an important day for her. She was starting a class on Saturday to help improve her writing skills and get into a good college.

Sunday came quickly. Gabby was scheduled to work at the library that afternoon. She caught herself constantly looking at the door for Aaron. Lots of people came in that day, but not Aaron. Maybe he has already forgotten me; the young woman dwelled in self-pity.

Her shift was finally over. She left the library and slowly walked toward the bus station. There were not many people on the streets at that time, as usual. Suddenly someone touched her shoulder; she was ready to scream. Then she turned and she saw Aaron's welcome and familiar dark face, and, particularly, his burning eyes. He kissed her gently without offering any explanations or excuses; then he handed her a single red rose. This simple gesture broke down her defenses. Gabby smiled. All was well, all was forgiven.

She was ready to be his lover right then and there. Good thing he had not asked her yet. *"Why is he not asking me? Maybe he does not like me as much,"* she mused. Aaron did not know what storm was clouding Gabby's beautiful mind as he was holding her, kissing her.

The nights were getting colder. "Do you want to come to my place? It is cold here," he said. Gabby wanted to scream "yes!" but she knew better. Her Mom and her grandmother warned her a long time ago never to put herself in a situation where she would be alone with a man. Her girlfriends, some of whom already had more experience than she will ever have, taught her to be careful. Do not give in too quickly to his requests, because the man will think that she is just an easy girl. Gabby's modest upbringing was preventing her from doing something her body was longing to do. "Maybe another time," Gabby answered softly.

Then Aaron kissed her even more passionately, on the lips. After that, he started kissing her neck slowly. She unbuttoned her coat. His big hands landed on her breasts. Gabby was gasping for air. She was kissing his hands, his face; she buried her fingers in his curly hair. *This has to stop,* she caught herself thinking. But his hands did not stop exploring her body.

Finally, Gabby separated herself from him. Her pulse was racing, she felt lightheaded and warm. Aaron was just smiling; he did not ask her for more, and yet…

They walked slowly to the bus station. The bus was late, as usual. Her hands were getting cold. *I should have taken my gloves,* Gabby thought. Aaron slowly started kissing her left hand, and then her right hand. He was tracing her fingers with his hot lips. Gabby closed her eyes. *Please, bus, come quickly,* she said to herself. Her prayers were heard! The old red-and-black bus was slowly approaching. She was about to say goodbye, when Aaron hopped onto the bus with her. Noticing the surprised look in Gabby's eyes, he said quietly in his deep voice, "I want to see where my girl lives."

"He called me his girl!" Gabby said to herself, as her heart was singing.

Not too many people were riding the dimly lighted bus at this time of the night. The couple took seats at the back of the bus, where was even darker and no one else was sitting. Aaron started kissing her passionately again, but Gabby's body stiffened. "Please, don't kiss me here. Some people on the bus might know my parents." Her pleading did not stop him, however. The young man's hand slowly got under her coat, and then under her skirt. He found her warm, moist place. His fingers were moving skillfully. Gabby took a deep breath, then covered her mouth to mute the sound of her moaning. "Aaron, please!" she was mumbling. At the same time, they both felt the warm gushing that was coming from her body, on his hand. She turned to him and smiled; he smiled back. Gabby had never felt this way. Is this what is described as reaching climax? She did not know, and she did not dare ask him.

It took Gabby time to put her clothes and her emotions back in order. But then the bus had finally arrived at her neighborhood. She stood up, dressed properly, and was ready to say goodbye to him again. Aaron smiled and shook his head, saying firmly, "No. I am coming with you." Gabby gave him a scared look while he took her hand and guided her toward the bus exit.

When they had almost reached her house, Gabby turned to him and said, "You cannot come any closer. If my father sees you…" But she did not finish the sentence.

"I will not come closer, my love. I just wanted to be sure that you had reached your home safely." Aaron kissed her again, gently, on the lips. "Good night, my love."

She turned the key in the lock and looked back. He was standing there, smiling. *How will he get home*, she wondered? It was getting late and few buses ran at this time. She waved at him. Her heart was singing, and her eyes were smiling when she entered the living room. "Someone gave my daughter a rose," her father said to her playfully. Gabby realized she was still holding the rose Aaron had given her. She went to look for a vase to try to hide her embarrassment. Tonight's events were fresh in her memory. She was hoping nobody had seen their mini love-making on the bus, and that her behavior would not be reported to her father later

5

Taking the Next Step

"Picking at rose petals, watching them drop;
she loves me or she loves me not"

–J Boog (Born August 11, 1985), American reggae and
R&B vocalist and songwriter.

It was difficult for Gabby to fall asleep that night. Never before in her young life had she had an issue concerning falling, or staying, asleep. Her mind was constantly playing the unbelievable events of the evening over and over again. *He gave me a rose*, she thought with a sweet smile. Yes, the young girl had received flowers from her suitors in the past. But none of those bouquets made such a significant impression on her like the single red rose she had received from Aaron tonight. This rose had a very symbolic meaning to her. Roses were her favorite flowers; Rose was her mother's name; the rose was the symbol of her country and a source of the famous fragrant Bulgarian rose oil. Gabby always kept a vial of that oil in her purse. She loved the smell because it reminded her of her grandmother's beautiful garden.

Suddenly Gabby stood up and took the rose from the vase. She lay back down on her bed, the flower in her hand. She started tracing her entire body with the fragrant blossom, closed her eyes and let her imagination run wild. She could almost feel Aaron's strong hands touching her all over. What a night!

"He said that I am his girl. He called me 'my love!'" Hadn't she read recently in a book about a woman with a vivid imagination? How did the story end? She could not remember now, and, besides, it was not that important anyway. Life is much more exciting than the books she reads. Maybe she would even start writing in a diary again, if she can find time in her busy schedule.

The following week, Gabby buried herself in her studies and her work. A few times, she caught herself daydreaming. Aaron was busy all week at the University as well. She learned from him during their last meeting that he graduates from Medical School in a few years. He did not talk about his future plans, however. What was he going to do after he graduates?

By now, Gabby had learned to trust her gut feelings. She strongly sensed that there was something important that this man was not revealing to her.

Aaron did not come around, looking for her, at the library this week. She had given him her phone number when they met for the second time; but he had not called her. Neither her parents nor her sisters had mentioned anyone asking for her on the phone. Gabby started feeling a bit anxious. At the beginning of a love story, it is difficult to stay away from the one you love, a feeling similar to the compulsion drug addicts have when they do not get their daily dose. Well...Gabby had not had her daily dose of Aaron's sweet kisses and touches, and she was definitely craving more.

When she went to her job in the library on Friday afternoon, one of her co-workers gave her a hand-written note from Aaron. What beautiful handwriting he has! *I know that we have a few books in the library on graphology. I must find them now and decode what secrets his note is holding*, she thought to herself. He had come to the library to find her, yet he did not wait for her?! What could possibly keep him away from her—except his studies, of course? Aaron wrote that he plans to see her on Saturday, late afternoon, if she is available. He set the time and place for the meeting. She was not used to boys taking charge! She wondered, *Do I like this, or not?*

Gabby could not wait for Saturday late afternoon to come! She attended her morning class as usual. While riding the bus home from the class, she mentally went over all the clothes in her small closet. Nothing seemed to be suitable for the occasion! She does not own the type of clothes her girlfriends considered "sexy." After returning home, she felt so anxious that she barely ate lunch. In the afternoon, she had a confrontation with one of her little sisters who had taken, and worn, Gabby's favorite sweater. She had hoped to wear that sweater tonight. Now the sweater needed to be washed, so Gabby was not going to be able to wear it. Finally, after washing and drying her hair, Gabby decided to wear her old red blouse with a black pencil skirt. She would love to add some color to her outfit, in anticipation of the "big night," or at least, she was hoping tonight would be the big night.

Red was Gabby's favorite color, because it complements her dark eyes, her dark hair, and her white skin. Gabby chose to put on a new pair of black stockings—a rare luxury for girls at that time. Those stockings would make her feel sexy, which will remove the feeling of dissatisfaction growing in her created by the fact that she had to wear once more the only coat and only pair of boots she owns—her school uniform coat and black boots. Both the coat and the boots were old, worn, and a bit outdated. Gabby hated her school uniforms and absolutely disliked wearing dark colors, especially during the winter months. Dark colors represent to her the idea of death and mourning.

Gabby sighed; she had been dreaming for a long time about wearing red shoes, or red boots with heels. Dark navy blue and black were the only colors students were allowed to wear at her school. So, it was not practical for the shoemakers of that time to produce shoes of different colors in big quantities. Maybe she would be very lucky, and one day one of her parents' friends who travels abroad will bring her a pair of shoes in her favorite color, red, from another country.

When Gabby finds rare moments free from school and work time, she loves to sit in her Aunt Ani's living room and go through this enormous catalog from Neckermann in Germany. Those were her stolen moments of happiness and dreaming of fantasies. Although she knew the beautiful items in the catalog by heart, she still enjoyed looking at them—the beautiful clothes, shoes, underwear, furniture, small gadgets and household items. Is this all real? Are there countries in the world where people actually live like this? The idea that a regular person could shop freely at any given store, without having to wait outdoors in a line for hours, and then actually get what she wants and likes was all so foreign to her. During those moments, it was difficult for Gabby to shake off her dreaminess and return to her real, much more difficult and drab, life than that depicted in the catalog.

Finally on that late Saturday afternoon, Gabriella was satisfied by the image of the beautiful young and sophisticated girl she saw swirling in front of the mirror. She was debating whether to put on a little make-up. Her sister was circling around Gabby, asking questions: "Where are you going? Why are you dressed like you are having a date?" Her sister's teasing was the last straw that just added to Gabby's huge anxiety. She left the house one hour earlier than the set-up time for the date, to walk and clear her head before seeing Aaron.

What was she expecting to happen tonight? Was she really ready to take this step? Gabby was a virgin. Her head was full of romantic stories from the thousands of books she had read. None of them seemed to prepare her for real life, and especially for tonight's event. How should she behave? What would she say? Was he going to know that was her first time? Is it going to be painful? Will she bleed? How about if she gets pregnant?! Her Mother was constantly warning her about this danger. No, he is older than she, so he knows what to do. And, he is a medical student, after all. They teach these things at the University.

She wished she had someone to talk to about her fears. Talking to her Mom was, of course, out of the question. All her girlfriends claimed they had lost their virginity a long time ago. She was embarrassed to admit to them that she had not yet. So, she would keep all these questions for herself and behave like an experienced girl.

Aaron was already waiting for her at the Clock Tower, a favorite place for daters to meet. He said he lived not far away, then asked if she would like to take a stroll along the city's commercial street? Gabby had already walked for about an hour earlier, so she said, "No. Let's go to your place." Since she was supposed to be this experienced girl, after all, she had to give the impression that she was not at all scared. The young man smiled, then hugged and kissed her gently. Gabby's fears started to melt away. He is gentle, he loves me; he will make the evening go smoothly.

They were climbing a heavenly-looking marble staircase inside an old building. Gabby was enjoying the architectural details everywhere, and was tracing with her fingers the figures on the ivory marble ledge. Aaron stopped and showed her an apartment door, Number 7, on the second floor. "This is my family's apartment. My parents live here."

"And where do you live?" Gabby inquired. He smiled, and gently pushed her to walk further upstairs. He was taking her to his place—in the attic! It was actually common at that time for an adult man who still lives with his parents to occupy an attic that was remodeled as a small apartment.

Gabby was surprised to see how well-organized and clean his space looked. Had he cleaned especially because of her visit, or was he an organized person in general? This distinction was not so important to learn tonight, however.

Once inside his apartment, Aaron gently pushed her to the wall and started kissing her passionately; her body temperature rose immediately. She pushed him away and smiled. "What a gentleman you are! Let me take off my coat first!" He complimented her on her appearance. To the black-and-red ensemble, Gabby had added a pair of small red earrings shaped like roses. As he was tracing her little ears with his tongue, she pushed him away again. "Aren't you going to offer me something to drink?"

The young man brought out two glasses and half a bottle of cognac. The amber-looking liquid felt smooth, like velvet in her throat. Gabby had had almost nothing to eat that day, so the drink quickly made her feel dizzy. Her anxiety, however, was starting to vanish as her body relaxed. The two were sitting on the bed now; he was taking her clothes off, one by one. She was holding his head and passionately kissing his face.

Then she was lying on his bed, naked. She did not feel awkward; she knows she has a beautiful young body, perhaps a little curvy. Aaron was looking at her with adoring eyes, touching every curve of her body, covering her entirely with kisses. Her neck, her shoulders, her nipples, her navel, the little spot between her thighs and her pubis. She was moaning with delight. Gabby was inhaling his smell, hugging him, bringing his body close to her. She did not have the knowledge of experience, but her natural instincts were guiding her.

She clearly felt when he entered her, and she screamed out. His eyes widened. "No, don't stop," she cried. She was moving her body in perfect synchrony with his thrusts. Their young bodies were entangled, sweaty; their lips were swollen from so many kisses; their hearts were beating incredibly fast.

He suddenly collapsed on top of her. Was that all? She wanted more! She did not want to separate her body from his.

Then she saw the bright moon appearing on the roof, at the corner of the skylight. The moon and the universe were witnessing their passionate love-making! She was playing with his curly hair; she loved his curls, so soft to the touch, and very fragrant. She felt the warmth of his body all over hers. He smiled sweetly at her and reached for his cigarettes, observing, "I didn't know if you smoke."

"Sometimes I do. Do you want me to try it?" She inhaled the smoke and felt calm immediately take over her senses.

They stayed in bed for an hour, smoking and drinking. Both were naked, which felt very natural. She was comfortable being around him, as if she had known him for a long time. How long had it actually been? Only a few days had passed since they met, but she felt he was definitely an important part of her life already.

He stretched out his hands and got his guitar, adjusted the strap and started strumming and singing in a low voice about roses and love. *"Didn't you say that you wanted to hear me singing?"* he teased her.

"No, you asked me if I wanted to hear you singing," Gabby laughed her vibrant laugh.

I wish this moment would last forever, Gabby thought. *But I have to get dressed and go back home.*

6

Graduation, and the Beginning of a Busy Summer

"What lies behind you and what lies in front of you, pales in comparison to what lies inside of you"

> – Ralph Waldo Emerson (1803-1882), an American essayist, lecturer and philosopher. Emerson was a poet and an abolitionist who led the transcendentalist movement of the mid-19th century. He has dozens of published essays and made more than 1,500 public lectures across the United States.

Aaron and Gabby had been dating steadily for about six months already. They met regularly at his attic apartment, two or three times a week. Each time they saw each other, he made passionate love to her. She stopped worrying about getting pregnant after he showed her his drawer full of condoms; and he followed through on his promise to use them each time they made love. Some days Gabby wondered why he needed to have so many in that drawer, but she quickly chased those thoughts away from her mind.

Tonight, they were lying naked in his bed again after making love. He was singing one of the few songs he had written about her. Gabby was smoking, listening and smiling. She was happy and content. Life is easy when one is young and in love!

They were talking about going to the beach tomorrow, the beginning of June. Both of them were going to have a difficult month ahead. Aaron had to take five exams at the end of this semester. Gabby was traveling to the capital of Bulgaria soon to take two entrance exams in order to be admitted to the Journalism Department at the University. So, they were taking every available minute to be together now.

A few weeks ago, it was Gabby's prom night. She invited Aaron to her house and introduced him to her parents. Her father did not look happy to learn that the boy was Jewish, but seemed to like him anyway. Miho invited Aaron to sit at the dining table and drink with him. This was a clear sign of acceptance. That day, her Mom was too busy with cooking and serving dinner for the relatives and friends to pay much attention to Aaron. Graduations and proms are a big event in Bulgaria, as important as weddings.

Gabby chose to be dressed for prom night in a white bell lace dress, with red trimming and a red belt. Her hair was skillfully done up in a sophisticated bun. The hairdresser even used a few real red roses. Gabby's mother Rose cried from sheer joy when she saw her grown-up daughter dressed like a magazine cover girl. This reminded Rose of her wedding day. So, she decided to share with her daughter the story about getting the gorgeous piece of fabric from her girlfriend for her wedding gown. *Why are you telling me this story today, Mom? This is not my wedding day! There will be time to share the story with me in the future,* Gabby thought. But her mother's heart somehow sensed what lay ahead for Gabby. *Maybe my first-born daughter will end up unmarried,* Rose thought to herself.

Gabby kissed her Mom and Dad goodbye. She and Aaron drove to the restaurant in the luxury car borrowed from her father's friend, which was the custom at that time. The restaurant was in the nearby tourist complex. It was a tradition at that time for the prom to be held at big restaurants. After dinner, Gabby and Aaron were spending the night in a hotel room. This was their first official night together, the first one her parents knew about.

All of Gabby's classmates were dressed in a very fashionable way. Their teachers were invited to the prom dinner at the restaurant as well. It was an unforgettable night for everyone: their first night as adults. The former students and their teachers were dancing, laughing, and remembering all the school years. Gabby's girlfriends, who were charmed by Aaron's gentlemanly behavior, all told Gabby she is lucky to have met him. The young woman was smiling for their prom picture together, proud of her beauty and her choice of man.

Gabby was lying on a towel on the sand at one of her favorite beaches. Aaron was swimming in the warm seawater not far from her; she could see his masculine body glistening in the sun during his laps. She was holding a book in her hands, but her mind was not on the book. Aaron had just told her that she was invited next Sunday to a family lunch at his house. A lunch with his parents! This was an important event.

Many times, during those six months of dating him, Gabby wondered why she had not yet received this invitation. Now, she was not sure whether she should be happy, or concerned. She knew a bit about Aaron's parents from him. His father was a prominent lawyer in the city, and his Mom was an accountant. They had two sons. Aaron has a younger brother, who wanted to study medicine as well when he gets older. This information was not enough, however, to predict how the lunch would unfold.

Aaron lay down on the beach towel next to Gabby. He kissed her; his lips were salty from the sea, his body slippery and wet. His eyes were smiling only at her. His fingers were tracing her body, warm from the sun. "Aaron, please, people are looking at us," she whispered in his ear.

"Let them look," he teased her. Gabby stood up and started to get dressed. They were going to meet for dinner tonight with a group of his friends from the University, and she wanted to make a good impression.

The group was meeting at a fish restaurant. There were many of those small places, which had been built in a hasty manner around the beach boulevard. They usually served freshly caught local fish, mostly European sprat. The fish was served fried, with chips as a side. Customers usually order local beer to go with the fish. The food was cheap, but tasty, and the atmosphere was authentic. Any day of the week during the summer months those restaurants were filled with lots of clients, and were favorite spots for college students.

The night was warm, filled with the tantalizing smell of the Black Sea. The voices and laughter of the young people were echoing everywhere.

Gabby felt uncomfortable around Aaron's friends, since she was the youngest one in the group. They were all medical students, and their chatter about diseases, professors and lectures made her feel inadequate and immature. Aaron was having a good time and seemed oblivious to her discomfort. She would have much preferred to spend this night alone with him in his small attic apartment. He hugged and kissed her in front of everybody. But she felt embarrassed. His breath smelled of beer; he was getting drunk.

Gabby suddenly felt the urge to go home. Aaron called a cab for her, but then decided to stay with his friends. They kissed goodbye coldly. Gabby cried in the taxi all the way to her house.

"Why did he behave in such a way? He was so cold! Didn't he understand how important it was for me to spend time with him alone tonight?" For the first time, she was questioning his feelings and motivations. It was sometimes not easy to love him, and to understand his actions. *"Well, the morning is smarter than the night."* Gabby recalled the famous Bulgarian proverb.

Aaron called the next morning, very apologetic about letting her go home alone last night. He said he was starting to study diligently for his exams and would see her on Sunday at his parents' apartment for lunch. What choice did she have but to accept his explanation about why they could not see each other the other night?

A few days passed without her seeing him. Gabby filled the time with her studies and with long, lonely walks in the nearby forest. One time she went to the beach alone. She recalled the last time she and Aaron were happy at this same place. The feeling of missing him overwhelmed her, and she left the beach in a hurry.

Saturday night came quickly. The young woman's delicate soul was filled with anxiety and gloomy premonitions. She did not even have a desire to choose her clothes carefully for lunch, which was unusual for her organized nature. Before any important event, Gabby usually laid out her ironed clothes, and washed and styled her hair as well.

But tonight was different. She was thinking about the possibility of not showing up to lunch at all tomorrow. After giving much consideration to this, she decided to attend the event after all. It is not polite for someone to simply not show up if one has been invited to lunch or dinner. That would violate the unwritten Bulgarian social ethics code. She and Aaron would certainly discuss these issues after lunch.

7

The Lunch

"My children, borrow on My account and celebrate the holiness of the day and trust in Me, and I will repay"

(Betz.15b) Shabbat table song

The table in Aaron's parents' dining room was covered with a velvet tablecloth in a gold color. Gabby was seated away from Aaron. The table was brimming with food. Although Gabby was not familiar with most of the` dishes, she was determined to try them all.

The young woman was dressed in a very modest way. Gabby had let down her long, dark hair. She was looking and feeling like Snow White—an innocent young woman ready to be crushed by the evil Queen—in this case, Aaron's mother, who was giving a false impression of being an ordinary housewife. She was busily bringing more food in from the kitchen, and politely declined Gabby's offer to help. The older woman was dressed in green, with a tastefully wrapped scarf around her curly dark-brown hair. Her name was Rebecca, and she was very distinguished-looking. Gabby thought that the woman had probably been very beautiful in her youth.

Aaron's father was not a large man. Gabby somehow expected him to be tall, due to his reputation of being a fearless lawyer. Because he both had a moustache *and* was balding, that combination made his appearance a bit comical. He was very polite, asked Gabby lots of detailed questions about her future studies in the Capital, and seemed to like her answers. The man had a good sense of humor and shared some funny stories of his days in college, which made the palpable tension between Aaron's mother and Gabby less obvious.

Aaron's little brother was about ten years old and almost a carbon copy of Aaron! He looked like a very polite child, but Gabby detected mischievous twinkles in his eyes. He was looking at her with curiosity. Gabby wondered if she was the first girl Aaron had brought home.

Her love, the apple of her eye, Aaron, was unrecognizable around his parents, or as Gabby started to suspect, mostly so around his mother. Where was the bold young man she had met at the library months ago? Today, he was coy and quiet. Gabby met his gaze a few times but could not read his facial expression. They really do need to talk after lunch. She wanted to go to his apartment, or for a walk, just to be alone with him. They had not seen each other for a week, after all.

"How did you like the knishes?" Rebecca's melodic voice startled Gabby.

"I like them very much. They remind me of a pastry my grandmother used to bake." Gabby saw the patronizing look Rebecca gave her, but decided to ignore it.

Rebecca asked her younger son to go to his room right after lunch was over. Gabby's heart sank; she knew that the real reason for the visit was about to be revealed. She was sure that she had not been invited just to taste the delicious food Aaron's mother had prepared. His father was polite enough to offer her coffee, since Gabby had recently started drinking coffee. In her parents' home, children and young people were only allowed to have tea or milk. So Gabby was enjoying her cup of Joe as she patiently waited for Rebecca to speak.

Gabby was correct to expect Aaron's mother to take charge. His father was the famous lawyer, but his mother was in charge of the family. Aaron had revealed this family dynamic to her a long time ago.

Rebecca finally sat down at the table; she seemed tired, and was slowly sipping from her glass of chilled white wine. Finally, she looked Gabby straight in the eyes and started her soliloquy. The family likes Gabby. Nevertheless, Aaron needs to focus on his studies. After he graduates from the Medical University, instead of being sent into a small town or village to work a few years as a doctor (as mandated by the Bulgarian government at that time), the entire family will immigrate to Israel.

Aaron is engaged to the daughter of a famous surgeon in Haifa. His future father-in-law will help him establish his own practice. Aaron's parents do not mind if his son's relationship with Gabby continues, as long as she understands that there will be no plans for marriage. She is not a Jewish girl; she must understand that, for Aaron's family, keeping the Jewish tradition is important. Rebecca emphasized the sacrifices they as parents have made for their son. The unspoken truth behind her words was that Aaron's parents (especially his Mother) will not let some ordinary young girl destroy the carefully planned future of their son. Rebecca even had the audacity to insinuate that, since Gabby is leaving soon to be in a college herself, in another town, she might very well meet someone else there.

Gabby was listening, and her body was there, but her mind went back to the first time she had met the young man. How much he had impressed her with his handsomeness and his polite behavior. Now she slowly turned her gaze to Aaron, expecting him to say or do something. He only lowered his eyes and did not look at her. She had lost her desire to talk to him or to see him in private after lunch.

Gabby stood up and said that she understands. She thanked Rebecca for the lunch, said goodbye to everyone and quickly left the room, almost wanting to run down the elegant marble staircase. How much she used to love those stairs when they were leading her up to the attic!

She needed to walk and clear her mind. Rose had taught her early on that physical activity, fresh air and sun are the best cure for any physical or mental problems. *"I need my Mom now!"* Gabby cried inside. *"No, Gabriella, you are not a little girl any more. You have to go through this on your own."*

"Aaron is engaged!" Rebecca's words were echoing in Gabby's head. Pictures of their love-making were playing in slow motion in her brain. How, and why, had he never mentioned anything to her about moving to Israel?! From the beginning, she felt that he was hiding something; but never in her wildest fears had she imagined him being engaged. Was she just someone he was passing time with until his fiancée appeared? Did he ever love her, or had she just assumed that?

Gabby felt the warmth of the tears streaming down her face. Clearly devastated, she noticed a sharp pain in her chest that almost made her stop breathing. *Is this what people describe as "a broken heart?" Why do those feelings hurt so much? Am I going to recover from this awful betrayal?*

Gabby hastened her steps. She needed to go home and start packing for her trip to the Capital. She will be leaving in a few days, traveling on the train by herself for the first time. What if her parents ask her where Aaron is? Why is he not at the train station to say goodbye? She could not lie to them. Gabby sighed. It was going to be a difficult conversation with her Mom and Dad.

PART III

1

It Is an Exam Time

"There is no time for regrets.
You've just got to keep moving forward."

– Mike McCready (Born December 18, 1968), American entrepreneur in the music industry, CEO of Music Xray, a blogger on Huffington Post and a musician.

The scenery from the window of the train was spectacular. Gabby enjoyed looking at the lush golden wheat fields and the little houses in the villages the train passed on its path. She was traveling to Sofia, the Capital, on this sunny summer day, to visit her parents' friends for a few days. They live in the Capital, and it was very convenient for her to stay in their house, which was close to the University. In two days, she was supposed to start taking her entrance exams for the Journalism Program.

Gabby was feeling calm and confident, because she had studied diligently, for a long time, and had taken classes for writing and literature for almost a year. She even wrote a couple of articles for the local newspapers, so she could claim that she has some relevant experience. For the exams, initially Gabby must write an essay on one subject in Bulgarian literature. After her essay is rated, if her score is high enough, she will continue by taking a special written exam on a contemporary subject of journalism. Then, if she passes that part, she will have a face-to-face interview with the professors. She was not scared of any of this; rather, she was ready for the challenge!

Aaron came to her mind often, but she was gradually chasing his image, and its accompanying memories, away. She made her final decision, not to see him before she left, because she needed to be centered now, to move forward with her life. The few years that lay directly ahead are significant for her future. He belongs to her past. Aaron's future is secured. She does not belong there, according to his mother. And he has not done anything to make her think otherwise. She was hurting inside; her trust and her love had been betrayed. Her feelings for Aaron were still raw, but she needed to bury them now and think clearly about herself. There was no time for self-pity.

Gabby arrived at Central Station in late afternoon. She found a pay phone and called Maria, her mother's longtime friend, wrote down the address and decided to splurge on a taxi. That area of the town was unknown to her, and she did not want to get lost. She was tired after the long trip, and wanted to take a shower and then rest as quickly as possible.

Gabby was warmly greeted by Maria, a woman in her fifties with a motherly look. She served her a tasty home-cooked meal and encouraged her to go to bed early. The next morning, however, Gabby woke up late. She had planned to review some of the books for the last time, and to take a long walk. The day after this was the start of the exams.

The two women chatted a bit while drinking their morning coffee. Gabby told Maria the news about her parents and her sisters, then showed her some pictures of the graduation. Maria shared the news about her children. After that, Maria was in a rush to get to work, so Gabby was alone in the big house. She chose to study in one of the brightest rooms, where the sunlight was streaming through the big window, and devoted a few hours of the day to her studies.

In the afternoon, Gabby took a short nap and left the house for a walk in the neighborhood, one of the oldest parts of Sofia—the Bulgarian Capital. The old gray buildings, which had lots of architectural details, were peacefully coexisting with the newly built multi-level establishments made of glass and steel. Most of the paved streets are lined with big, old chestnut trees on both sides. People were out taking their daily walks, and the streets were booming with life. Later in the day, the evening breeze from the nearby mountain, Vitosha, made the summer's heat more bearable.

Gabby liked the atmosphere in this place. She was charmed by the symbiosis of the old way of life and the new vibrant, artistic life. If she passed her exams successfully, it might be nice to rent a small apartment, or even a room, in this part of town. She felt she would be able to live here, in harmony with both herself and the world at large. Gabby sighed. It was, however, way too early to make plans for the future. The difficult part ahead, passing the exams, was just starting.

The following morning, she woke up early. She had a small but filling breakfast and a coffee with Maria again. Before Gabby left the house, the older woman spilled some water from a big jar in front of her. This turned out to be an ancient Bulgarian tradition that is still followed to this day. The symbolic meaning is to bring good luck to a person who is starting an important event or going on a journey.

To get to the University, Gabby had to take a trolley. She had never ridden in a trolley before. The streetcar was crowded with people. Gabby likes to observe people when she is riding a bus or a train; she enjoys making up stories about the passengers' lives. Today, she wondered if the young people traveling with her were going to the University as well, to take the same exam? How many of them will be competing against her?

Gabby got off the trolley and crossed the street, as did many of the other trolley passengers. She was right, after all—most of the young people were going to take that exam as well. The impressive main building of the University emerged in front of her. This was an old, magnificent, yet a bit pompous, campus, with a few marble columns standing around its entrances. The main entrance had two big three-dimensional sculptures of the influential founders of the University. Gabby will learn their names soon, as well as the detailed history of this famous Alma Mater for generations of Bulgarians.

She did not enter through the main entrance but, rather, followed the signs and entered the building from the back. All the possible future students were directed to a big auditorium, whose seats were organized like an amphitheater. Gabby took a number from the table located next to the entrance door, then chose a seat in the middle of the auditorium. Everyone was given a few stamped pieces of paper and a pencil. The students were not allowed to talk to each other. If they had a question, they were supposed to raise one hand and talk quietly with the observers. The atmosphere in the auditorium was full of tension. Most of the young people's faces looked stressed, due to their anxiety about the exam. Gabby, however, was calm. The chosen subject seemed easy to her, and she started writing speedily.

The two hours allowed for writing passed quickly. Her back, however, was hurting from the uncomfortable wooden chair. So she left the building and decided to take a long walk. Gabby had visited the Capital a few times in the past, but was never alone, and always had to follow someone else's schedule. Now she was finally free to roam the town at her own pace, and to familiarize herself with the streets, buildings, churches, and museums. The city was much bigger than her hometown and was full of life and people. She saw a small farmers' market across the street, where she bought some succulent-looking red and white cherries. June was the season for cherries, salads, green onions and green garlic. Gabby loves all the fruits and vegetables that grow in the fertile land of her country.

After her long walk, Gabby came back to Maria's house. The rest of Maria's family had just arrived back from a short trip out-of-town. They were very happy to see Gabby, and lots of hugs and kisses were exchanged. Everyone was asking her about her parents, her sisters, and graduation day; they also wanted to know how the exam went today. This big family reminded Gabby of her own family. So, while waiting for dinner to be prepared, she called home. Rose asked lots of questions about her trip and about today's exam. The Bulgarian mothers, like any other mothers in the world, were always concerned about the well-being of their children, especially when they were far away. The family had prepared a feast in Gabriella's honor. They all sat outside the house in the yard. The night sky was full of stars, and the moon was resplendent. Her mother's friend's warm love and genuine care was palpable. Gabby was able to chase away for a while the painful memories of Aaron, and her concerns about the results of the exams. She enjoyed herself, Maria and her family, and this warm, beautiful summer night.

2

Gabby Has Been Accepted
to the University

"Nothing is impossible;
the word itself says, 'I'm possible'!"

– Audrey Hepburn, (1929–1993), British actress and humanitarian. Recognized as both a film and fashion icon, Audrey Hepburn was ranked by the American Film Institute as the third-greatest female screen legend from the Golden Age of Hollywood.

A long line of students crowded outside the University. A big bulletin board was posted on the wall with the names and the grades of the students who were accepted into the different programs. Gabby was reading the board for the second time. Her excitement was high, but she was not able to find her name among the other students' names. Finally, she saw it under "Students Accepted for the Journalism Faculty." Was it true?! She looked again. Yes, it was true! She was accepted! In her imagination, she wanted to run out onto the streets and shout from sheer happiness and relief. Of course, she actually did nothing of the sort.

What she did, however, was very unusual for her, or for any young person of the time. She went to the nearby small church and lit a candle. At that historical time period, religion was forbidden, and the religious holidays were not celebrated officially. Almost nobody was allowed to enter churches to participate in Liturgies, especially young people. This act could bring lots of trouble into her life. At that moment, Gabby did not think about the danger. This way of expressing her happiness and appreciation seemed appropriate to her.

She entered the empty church, which was alluring her with its cool calmness on this hot summer day. She loved the smell of the frankincense and the aroma of wax candles. The church was empty, with the exception of one old lady who was selling small religious symbols and books. Gabby asked her a few questions about where to put the lit candles, and about the proper way to pay tribute to the Saints depicted on the icons. The lady was happy to help her and to chat with someone.

Gabby was somehow familiar with the order in the church service. Her grandmother Dona arranged Gabby and her sisters to be baptized in the secrecy of their home when they were babies. Later, Dona put lots of efforts in teaching her grandchildren some of the basic history and rules of Christianity. She often took Gabby and her sisters to the church on important religious holidays. Older people in the country were unofficially allowed to participate in religious life.

Gabby took her time while looking at the faces of all the different Saints. She moved her lips in a silent prayer, then left the church in a very calm and peaceful mood. Life outside the church walls was still the same—busy and hectic, like every day.

Gabby went back to Maria's house to tell everyone the good news. She called home as well, but was only able to get one of her sisters on the phone. So, she left a message for her parents about her acceptance at the University and said that she would try to get a ticket on the night train in order to get back home in the morning.

Again, lots of kisses and hugs were exchanged between Maria's family members and Gabby. Promises were made to see each other during the summer vacation in August, or in the fall, when Gabby would start her first year as a University student.

The train ride back home was happier and less stressful than the previous trip. Gabby was full of plans for the rest of the summer, for the school year, and for her life ahead.

It was going to be a strange summer without Aaron, Gabby thought. She tried to keep herself occupied and busy, avoiding places that reminded her of him. Often, she went to the beach to sunbathe, since she needed to collect enough sunshine in her body to last during the cold winter months. Most of the time, she visited the beach by herself; at other times, she went with a big group of friends and former classmates. The majority of the young people in her circle of friends had been accepted to colleges or universities in different towns in Bulgaria. She was also happy that some friends would be studying in the Capital with her and wondering whom she should invite to be her roommate when she moved to the city of Sofia in the fall.

Summers in Bulgaria last only three months. For the people who live on the coast, this is the busiest time of year. The town's economy was booming. Because thousands of tourists from different countries were housed at the hotels and in private homes, local restaurants and hotels attracted young people from all over the country to work there during this season.

One of Rose's friends found a summer job for Gabby at the local hotel. At that time, it was very difficult to be accepted as an employee at the hotels visited by foreign tourists. One has to come from a reliable family and needs to be fluent in foreign languages. Gabby's fluency in the Russian language and basic knowledge of English made her a good candidate for the job of receptionist. She was thankful that she did not have to work night shifts, like the rest of the staff at the hotel, because of her age. On her days off, she would still have time to go to the beach and meet her friends. Gabby was very happy about this job also because it would allow her to save some money for the school year. She did not want to put a huge financial burden on her parents with her studies.

Gabby had a week-long job training that went very well. Today was her first shift working by herself, and she felt a bit fidgety. A big group of tourists from Israel had just arrived by bus from the airport. They needed to be accommodated with rooms as soon as possible and then eat a meal, because everyone wanted to get to the beach. She made a few minor mistakes, but basically was able to get the job done quickly and accurately. She could not help but wonder, when she looked at the faces of the young Jewish girls from the group, if one of them could be Aaron's fiancée.

After the tourists finished their lunch, one of the servers brought Gabby some delicious food. He was a charming young man and apparently had some interest in her. Gabby smiled while thanking him for the lunch. No, she knows she is not ready to date again. The wounds left by Aaron's engagement and his future departure for Israel had not yet healed.

Summer went by quickly. In August, Maria's family arrived in town for a short vacation. Gabby found a room for them at the hotel where she was working. They were very appreciative and took her with them during their car trips to nearby towns. Gabby especially liked to visit, whenever possible, the famous botanical Gardens at the nearby small coastal town of Balchik. The Garden itself was located on the premises of a former summer residence of a Romanian Queen. The place was magical; it was an oasis of calm and peace. Gabby was very attracted by the different types of flowers and trees. Her favorite, of course, was the rose garden; she also liked the cactus garden. Cacti often look elegant when they bloom.

Gabby was imagining how it would feel to have a wedding at such a beautiful place; to be dressed in white, surrounded by your family and friends, with classical music playing in the background. The young woman could see in her mind the familiar dark-complexioned face of the groom and his soft, curly hair. However, she quickly cast off those images of her former lover, Aaron.

It was one of Gabby's last days of work at the hotel in September. Most of the tourists were gone. She had volunteered to help clean and prepare the hotel for winter. Soon she would be leaving to start her studies at the University in Sofia.

The day's work was finished. Some of the employees were sitting in the lobby, chatting and drinking coffee—Gabby among them. She stood up and went to the reception desk to gather her belongings. Suddenly, something made her turn around. She was facing the glass entrance door of the hotel; it was Aaron, standing right there, looking at her.

Thousands of thoughts and words came to her mind. She wanted to scream at him, to tell him to go away, to leave her alone. But she simply waited until he approached her. "Let's go for a walk on the beach," Aaron suggested.

"Why?" Gabby was fighting to get control over her voice.

"I'm not going to take much of your time." The young woman said good-bye to her co-workers and followed Aaron out the door, ignoring their curious looks.

The sand on the beach was getting cooler, and the waves were rustling less. "You look different, Gabby," Aaron observed. She was quietly walking next to him. The young woman felt unusual, as if she had grown in the last few months. He shared that her sister had given him the information about Gabby's acceptance into the University, and the name of the hotel she is working at. *I know firsthand that Aaron does have this effect on women—younger, or older, he gets what he wants.* Gabby thought to herself. *I am definitely going to talk to that little Missy when I get home, about teaching her how to keep secrets.*

"Aaron, why are you here?" She turned toward him.

"I wanted to see you and to congratulate you on your acceptance at the University. I am happy that you have achieved your dream!"

"You could have congratulated me over the phone."

"I was in a hurry to see you because I knew that you were probably leaving soon for the Capital." The young man tried to take Gabby's hand.

"I am sorry, Aaron. I do not want you to touch me any more."

His eyes darkened as he looked at her with unbearable sadness. "Gabby, what we had was real; my feelings were sincere. I did not want to hurt you in any way. Yes, I should have told you that I am engaged, but you would not agree to be with me if I had. I have not seen the girl that I am engaged to. It was all arranged by my mother and by the girl's parents. I really love you, Gabby."

Gabby was observing Aaron's face from a distance, like a scientist observes his subject. Suddenly she realized that she was no longer in love with him. He was still dear to her heart, but the love was gone. She indeed had matured. The young woman smiled at him in a way she smiled at her friends. She thanked Aaron for the congratulations and said goodbye. He stayed on the beach for a long time, looking after his lost love.

Gabby went home and sat in the yard under the old fig tree that had witnessed the birth and growth of many generations in Ivanov's clan. She remembers how, as a child, her grandmother Dona was putting her to sleep under that same tree, while telling her tales of the old times. Gabby liked to read or to ponder, sitting in this favorite spot in the yard. Yes, Aaron was correct. She had achieved her dream, her desire to study journalism. She had both gained something momentous and lost something momentous during this last year of her young life. She had lost her first genuine love. But she slowly came to understand that there would be more loves to come in the future.

She was happy that she now felt free from the obsession she once had for Aaron. This welcome liberation made her feel powerful. She had loved, had been hurt, and had survived. The memories of their relationship, and his image, were no longer haunting her. They truly belonged to the past.

Gabby was definitely opening a brand-new page of her life story!

❧ **3** ❧

Who is Emma?

*"The whole purpose of education is
to turn mirrors into windows."*

– Sydney J. Harris (1917–1986), American Journalist and
prominent author for *Chicago Daily News* and, later, for
Chicago Sun-Times

On this rainy late November morning, Gabby woke up early. She sat at the window, holding her warm herbal cup of tea in one hand, observing the raindrops. She was petting Zoe—the calico-colored cat that belonged to her roommate Emma—with her other hand. Emma was still sleeping. It had been raining since yesterday. Gabby loves autumn, the rain, the cold, and the smell of wet leaves. Even when this season made her a bit melancholic, she still enjoyed it. She was fascinated by all the seasons; but in the fall and in the winter, nature was falling into a state of deep sleep. And the promise of the resurrection of Mother Nature from her slumber in the springtime was captivating to Gabby.

Gabby was satisfied with her life as a University student. She was fully devoted to her studies. She enjoyed it all: listening to the lectures, to the wisdom of her teachers, studying by herself at home, and the long hours spent researching and learning in the library. She was writing short articles in hopes of seeing them published soon in the newspapers. That had not happened yet, but she was not discouraged.

The young woman had developed a close relationship with Emma, whom she found accidentally. When Gabby went to register for the fall semester at the University, she saw on a bulletin board a few notices from people looking for a roommate. She was not sure what made her choose the note that said "Pet lovers only," and could never imagine how that simple handwritten note would change the course of her life.

After she and Emma agreed to be roommates, Gabby moved quickly into the two-bedroom apartment, in one of the centuries-old dilapidated buildings. The rent for her room was right for her. And she did not at all mind the gloomy-looking building, because it was in the desired neighborhood. She could walk to the University during any weather. Also, the apartment was not far from Maria's house, which Gabby visited once a week for dinner.

Emma was a bohemian; she brought a different perspective to Gabby's life. She was a second-year student at the Conservatory, with a unique, velvety voice. She could sing from the time she woke up until she felt asleep, which was usually long after midnight. The young woman had long, blond hair and the most extraordinary blue eyes, but most importantly, she possessed a generous and enthusiastic soul.

Even though the building was not in pristine condition, Emma's apartment, a gift from her deceased grandmother, was in very good shape. The place had an aristocratic character, with its big windows, a fireplace, plush carpets, an old piano, and chandeliers in every room. Gabby could not believe her luck; to get a room in such an apartment—and at an affordable price! Emma did not really need the money from the rent. She just liked to have someone around who could keep her company. Emma had not had much luck with her previous roommate, she told Gabby. So, when Zoe the calico cat accepted Gabby right away, Emma said that was a very good sign.

Gabby did not add lots of decorations to her already perfect-looking room—with the exception of a few pictures of her family and her old red, white and blue porcelain doll. Zoe seemed to be a very well-trained cat; so Gabby was not at all concerned that the animal would break one of her most precious possessions.

Gabby and Emma were the opposite, the Ying and the Yang, the blond and the brunette. Emma's extroverted nature needed the balance of the quiet, introverted demeanor of her new roommate. They quickly became close friends.

It was surprising how quickly they managed to work out their opposite characters and schedules. Gabby woke up early, attended her lectures, then shopped for groceries. Usually when she came home for lunch, Emma was just waking up. Since Emma was a good cook, she took upon herself the task of cooking for both. Gabby was good at cleaning, organizing and ironing. The apartment was always spotlessly clean, and organized like it was ready to be featured on the cover of a national home décor magazine. It was not an easy task, to keep up with Emma's messiness, but Gabby overlooked this part of her roommate's shortcomings. She appreciated Emma's loving heart and the heavenly-tasting dishes she created.

Looking in from the outside, one could wrongfully make the assumption that everything came to Emma effortlessly. The young woman, however, actually poured lots of work into her studies and into pursuing her dream of becoming a noted pop singer. Her parents, who were well-known in artistic society, had some influence on her, but Emma was living independently and following her own path.

Gabby was amazed to meet celebrities who just happened to be Emma's close friends and came to visit her. Musicians and others Gabby had seen on television since her early childhood were now guests in their apartment! Emma invited a different famous person each time to her weekly dinners. Gabby helped her with the cooking, and with organizing these evenings. She enjoyed the conversations, the music, and the informal bohemian atmosphere. The young women got tickets for lots of interesting concerts, theatrical and operatic premieres, and they were invited to gallery openings, dinners, and diplomatic events. Gabby was certainly living a full and interesting life.

Emma and Gabby talked to each other about their previous lovers. Gabby shared her painful experience with Aaron and his family. Emma was a beautiful and easygoing girl who made friends effortlessly. Gabby was surprised to learn that her roommate actually only had one boyfriend before—Angel. He left the country and emigrated to the United States. This could have brought lots of trouble to Emma's life if her parents did not have friends among government officials. No one at that time could legally emigrate anywhere in the world. If they somehow managed to do so, they could never return without being prosecuted and incarcerated. Their family reputation was damaged for all future generations.

Emma was dreaming of being reunited with her lover one day; a dream that seemed unrealistic to Gabby. But she did not have the heart to tell her friend that it was unlikely this event would ever occur.

The school year passed quickly. Gabby saw her parents and sisters only a few times during the winter and spring breaks. She could not wait to get back home to her family and to the Black Sea. Gabby liked the mountains that surrounded Sofia, in fact she made lots of trips to see some of the famous places there. But she could not live for a long time far from the sea. Once Gabby read in one of the many books in her home library: "He has sea water instead of blood in his veins," describing someone who was in love with the sea. This was, indeed, true for Gabriella.

Gabby planned to work again, during the summer, at the same hotel where she was employed last year. She already was an experienced worker, and it was not difficult for her to get her previous position back. The hotels were booked with tourists from all over the world, as they were the previous summer.

Gabby managed to get free time away from work for a week to go on a camping trip with Emma and few of her roommate's friends, at an isolated place near a beach lagoon. This was a new experience for Gabby, and she grew to like the lazy days spent at the beach with the group of influential young people—especially, the cool nights, when everyone sat around the campfire. They cooked simple meals such as baked mussels on a tin sheet over the fire, drank wine, sang songs.

When Gabby looked at some of the pictures from that camping trip, she thought, *I resemble a Gypsy woman.* She had lost weight; her skin was glowing with a dark golden tan from the sun, her hair was spiked with natural highlights; she wore long, colorful sundresses and skirts, and cheap jewelry.

The young men in her group of friends were attracted by her natural beauty, her inquisitive mind, and her humble behavior. Some men had tried to approach her, but failed, for Gabby's heart was closed. It was difficult for her to believe that she would be able to love again in the future.

Emma as well had a difficult time pushing away her suitors. She was the type of woman who draws crowds of men around her like a magnet because of her beauty, as well as her voice. She could not enter a room without being noticed immediately by everyone. People on the streets turned their heads to look at her. This situation bothered Emma, but sometimes worked miracles for her.

That summer, a producer from national television approached Emma while she was dining out with friends, and offered her a small role in a movie. Emma agreed, mostly because she was promised that in the movie she would also perform songs. Gabby was very happy for her girlfriend and went with her to the audition. Emma's voice and personality enthralled both the director and the cast. She easily got the role.

Gabby knew that Emma's acceptance of that role meant that they would not be able to see each other often during vacation time. So, she followed Emma's advice and used the rest of the summer to improve her own skills in speaking English by taking a class on her days off.

English was a difficult language for her to master, despite the fact that she had some basic knowledge from school. She became frustrated by her slow progress. However, thanks to Gabby's teacher, Rita, who was very patient and kind, she was able to improve quickly. Then she truly enjoyed this time that was devoted to ameliorating her language skills.

The summer was over before the girls knew it. Both Gabby and Emma were ready to go back to their studies, and to the active social life in the Capital.

❧ **4** ☙

The Change Is On Its Way

"Any change, even a change for the better, is always accompanied by drawbacks and discomforts."

> – Arnold Bennett, (1867-1931), English author, best known as a novelist. A prolific writer, Bennett completed 34 novels, seven volumes of short stories, 13 plays, and a daily journal of more than a million words.

The second year at the University started in a rather unusual way for Gabby. One small newspaper published a few of the articles she had written during the summer. After that, she was invited to work part time for that newspaper. This, in her eyes, was a huge success. A newbie, an unknown name, a provincial girl, Gabby was nonetheless slowly moving ahead with her career.

Emma finished filming her first movie, in which she played just a small role, but also sang the soundtrack. The movie was scheduled to be released around New Year's Day. Emma was happy, and proud of her first success. Both women were full of hope for their careers, and for the future.

In late fall of that year (1989), the world was starting to change. The Berlin Wall in Germany had fallen. All former Socialist countries had been swept by the tide of transformation. In November, sudden changes occurred in the Bulgarian political and economic systems. The social order as they knew it was collapsing before their eyes, and the growing turmoil in Bulgaria was unsettling.

Suddenly, Gabby found herself in the middle of every interesting event that was happening in society. She was writing articles, attending political meetings at the University, participating in strikes and demonstrations. Her introverted nature was slowly changing. Her name started to be recognized, and she was even asked to give public speeches during student strikes. Emma was invited to sing during those events.

Young people from all over the county were excited and invigorated. They truly believed that the system was changing for the better. The borders were opening. People were able to apply for visas to travel around the world. The older generation was more reserved and careful in accepting the changes, however. Gabby had a few heated political discussions with her grandfather when she went home for the country's first official celebration of Christmas. Ivan told her not to believe that all changes would be for the better. He warned her not to fully trust the new political leaders and always to exercise her own judgment. Gabriella tried hard to follow her grandfather's great advice throughout her entire life.

The economy, which was formerly controlled by the Communist party, was shifting to a market economy. Many people lost their secure jobs and benefits. Others, who were close to the former Government, became rich overnight by expropriating public funds. Since this situation had created significant tension in the society, honest and brave reporting was very much needed. Brand-new newspapers, radio and television stations were opening. True journalism became more important than ever for the nation.

Gabby applied to work at one of the newly opened radio stations. She was trying to balance her studies with her new job, as well as continuing to help Emma organize frequent dinners at their apartment. They had started inviting various types of guests at that time: not as many celebrities; more political activists.

The next winter, due to the incompetent economic policies led by the Government, there would be shortages of food and necessary supplies; staple products would be rationed. People would be standing in long lines outside the stores, beginning early in the morning, to get milk and bread. At that time, Gabby was trying hard to continue with her regular schedule of attending lectures, writing for the newspaper, and working at the radio station in the afternoon. Since Emma could not wake up early in order to go and get the needed ingredients for their dinners, the girls decided to discontinue them.

Emma's parents brought over food to the roommates once a week. Gabby's parents and grandparents also sent her food packages regularly. The situation had become so critical that one day Rose called Gabby and offered that she should come back home and postpone her studies. At that point, Gabby reassured her mother that she was not starving. Things were not that bad.

One evening, a few of Emma's friends came to visit, bringing wine and homemade traditional sausages. One of the men shared his plans to emigrate to the United States, where he could apply to continue his education abroad. After Emma listened carefully to his thoughts, she had the idea to pursue her education in the USA as well. She was also excited by the possibility of being reunited with her boyfriend! Emma convinced Gabby to apply for an American education as well. To Gabby, this plan sounded very unrealistic. She did not want to discourage her friend's hopes, so she allowed Emma to apply for both of them.

Gabby's life continued as usual, with her busy schedule. She had almost forgotten about Emma's plans for emigrating. One late afternoon, Gabby returned to the apartment and found Emma dancing, singing, waving a big stack of papers like a fan. "Guess what, Gabby? The applications to continue our education in the USA were accepted!" Emma cried out excitedly, laughing at the puzzled look on Gabby's face.

"Emma, really?!" Gabby shouted, unsure whether to be happy or not.

"We are going to need lots of money in order to continue our education abroad," Gabby, practical as always, worried aloud. Emma explained that she had spoken with her parents already. They promised to help their daughter with the necessary money. Emma found a solution for Gabby's tuition as well; she had applied for a scholarship. Also, a few American foundations in Bulgaria had just started working with businesses and citizens.

Gabby sat on the couch and sighed. She had lots of questions, and a few suggestions, about the situation. Her main observation was that she was neither emotionally nor mentally prepared to leave her parents and her country behind, even for a few years.

"Emma, are you sure you could face the emotional toll of being separated from your family?" Gabby's painful experience with Aaron had made her mature beyond her age. "My dear friend Emma, is it worth it to leave your entire family behind for a man?"

Emma quickly responded, "Gabby, you have never met him! If you knew him, you would never think this way. He loves me; and besides, I could always move back home if I need to."

Gabby noted a few flaws in Emma's logical thinking but decided to keep them to herself for now. She tried to approach Emma from a different viewpoint. "Emma, you had such a success with your first movie. Then you recorded a few songs for the radio. Your career is just starting. Do you think you will be offered such opportunities in the USA, as a foreigner who does not speak good English?!"

Emma was offended by her remark and turned her back, saying in a quiet voice, "Gabby, my English is perfect."

Gabby knew her roommate well. Emma was thinking carefully about everything her friend had just said. *Let me leave her alone for now. She is too excited to process the information correctly tonight,* she thought to herself.

Emma opened a bottle of their rapidly shrinking supply of quality white wine. The two girlfriends sat quietly in front of the fireplace, each immersed in her own thoughts, hopes, and plans.

❧ 5 ❧

Emma Is Leaving Bulgaria

"Everybody has to leave, everybody has to leave their home and come back so they can love it again for all new reasons."

> – Donald Miller (born August 12, 1971), American author, public speaker and business owner. Donald Miller is the CEO of StoryBrand, a marketing company. He is also an author of personal essays and reflections about faith, God, and self-discovery. His first *New York Times*-bestselling book was *Blue Like Jazz* (2012).

A few months had passed since the last conversation between Emma and Gabby. Emma was working diligently on finishing her fourth year at the Conservatory. She had applied to study music in one of the prestigious colleges in New York City; but first, she needed to pass a test in English proficiency. So, for a few months she took individual lessons that would prepare her for the test, and was very pleased when she passed on her first try.

Emma's next step would be to get a visa. She went to the American Embassy, because she needed to pass an interview there in order to get her student visa. At that time, there were long lines in front of all the Western foreign embassies in the Capital. The lines started in the early morning; some people waited entire nights there. The formerly closed borders were now open, and people were encouraged to take advantage of this huge change.

Gabby was about to finish her third year in University. She had already made up her mind not to accompany Emma to the USA. It was a hard decision to make, but she was sure it was the right thing for her to do at this time. She wanted to finish her education in Bulgaria first. There was the issue with money as well; Gabby's parents were not able to help her as much as Emma's parents did. Even if she got the scholarship, she would still need more funds. It was one thing to study music in a foreign country, and an absolutely different issue to be a journalist there. Gabby was happy with her current job at the radio station, which was providing her with money, as well as building her confidence and adding to her professional experience.

Emma offered that Gabby could continue living in the apartment until she graduated—this was a huge relief for Gabby. She could not imagine how she would find a new room or apartment during that time, when rents were rapidly going up. Also, she could not envision living with someone else as a roommate. Emma had a heart of gold—a typical Bulgarian saying.

But there turned out to be an ulterior motive behind Emma's decision to let Gabby stay in the apartment. For right now, Emma was leaving Zoe behind and Emma knew that

Gabby would take good care of her beloved cat. Emma's mother was suffering from multiple allergies, including cat dander, so it was out of the question to leave Zoe with her Mom. Emma was also hoping that later on, when Gabby would probably change her mind about living in the USA, she would bring the cat to Emma in New York.

On this sunny 24th day of May, the Bulgarians were celebrating their beloved Holiday of the Culture and Cyrillic Alphabet (script). Emma decided to engage fully in the activities. It might well be her last May 24 as a student. First-graders to college students participated in cheerful parades all over the country. There were musical bands, with teachers and children dressed in their best clothes, holding portraits of Saint Cyril and Saint Methodius, the creators of the Cyrillic alphabet, decorated with wreaths of flowers. The mood of the parade-goers was definitely *elated*.

Gabby was at the event as well, working as a reporter for the radio station. Emma passed by with a group of friends, and Gabby did interesting interviews with them. After the parade, they all went out to lunch and drinks at a crowded local restaurant. The downtown area was full of students and other young people who were celebrating the Holiday.

Gabby was starting to feel the pressure of simultaneously working and studying full-time. She needed to take a few days off from work to relax. Emma and she planned to get away for a weekend before the start of final exams for the year. They decided to take a short trip to Maria's house in the mountains of Rila, located in the West part of Bulgaria. The fresh air, the home-grown produce, and the home-cooked meals offered an excellent nurturing regimen. Emma was waking up late, as usual, but Gabby enjoyed waking early-morning walks around the rural area, breathing in the fresh air, and washing her face in the cold waters of the local river.

This mountain town was different from the village she grew up in. The houses looked more like little fortresses, with internal courtyards and gardens. People did not breed cows or sheep, like the households in her grandparents' village. Instead, herds of goats were everywhere. And the feta cheese and yogurt made from goats' milk tasted heavenly. Gabby and Emma returned to the city both well-fed and deeply rested.

Sensing that the time for separation was galloping toward them, the two young women were both emotional and retrospective. They tried to spend as much time together as possible. Emma sorted through her clothes and possessions, setting aside many items for Gabby, despite her friend's protests. "Emma, you are not leaving forever. Please keep your belongings," Gabby pleaded. Emma finally set the date for the trip at the beginning of August and bought her airplane ticket. Her school year in New York started in early September. She would only have one month to settle in with her boyfriend Angel and to familiarize herself with the city and the country. Emma was mostly exhilarated about these prospects. But Gabby was sensing that her close friend was not sharing all her concerns. Despite her easy-going demeanor, Emma would likely have a difficult time being away from her parents, friends and everything she had ever known. However, her choice was made, and there was no turning back.

The current school year at the University had finished. Gabby was going back to her hometown for the summer and had secured a summer job at one of the local radio stations. Gabby promised she would come back to the Capital, Sofia, when it was time for Emma to leave the country. But Gabby would really rather have said goodbye now; she knew how painful separating at the airport could be.

This summer vacation was different for Gabby than those in previous years. The usual charm of the summer was lost—her dearest friend was leaving.

The farewell scene at the airport was extremely emotional for both friends, and for Emma's parents. There were tears, laughs, promises, hugs, and kisses. Gabby stood there, watching until the airplane took off from the runway. She was still waving, even though she knew her friend could no longer see her. "Good luck, Emma. I will miss you dearly. We will meet again soon," Gabby said through sobs.

6

Gabby Moves Back Home to Varna

The days, months and years were passing slowly for Gabby, ever since her precious friend had left their native country to study in America. Emma wrote emails to Gabby and called her regularly. So Gabby was very well-informed about every little detail of her friend's life. She was living with Emma's pains, her successes and failures, was following the progress of her studies, and the course of her relationship with her boyfriend. Emma had always liked to take photographs of places and people, herself included, of course. Gabby thought that her girlfriend was quite photogenic. Emma emailed tons of pictures to her. Gabby made a collage of the best photos to hang in her room. Lying in bed, Gabby observed her friend's face, trying to decode if Emma was hiding something behind her smile. How did her dear friend handle life in a foreign country, and how does she get along with Angel?

Emma came back once to Bulgaria, during one summer vacation. She was the same beautiful, happy woman with a good heart. Living in a big city in a foreign country had changed her a bit, though. She seemed more mature now, more centered.

She brought many presents for everyone, as that was a Bulgarian custom. It was quite obvious that she missed her family and her friends dearly. But she was determined to fulfill her dream of becoming a singer. After living in the USA for a few years, however, Emma realized that this vision would not be as easy to achieve as she had thought. Her voice was improving; she was singing mostly at College events. She was making friends, connections, expanding her social circle, confident that success in singing would come to her sooner or later.

Gabby eventually graduated from the University with honors. She moved back to her parents' house with her wonderful cat, Zoe. It was not the right time, however, to bring the cat back to her beloved owner, since Emma and Angel were still living in the apartment complex, where pets were not allowed. They were planning to buy a house with a yard, and then get married soon.

Gabby was happy that Emma had proved her wrong. Sometimes even the wildest dreams can become reality, and people could reunite with their loved ones. Not often for Gabby, nearly forgotten memories about Aaron were surfacing in her mind. She wondered where he was now. Is he married? Does he have children? She had not seen any of his family members since she moved back to her hometown, assuming that they had moved to Israel as planned.

Rose and Miho opened a small family restaurant that provided a livelihood for the whole extended family. The restaurant served traditional Bulgarian dishes and was quite a success at that time. Gabby was working at one of the local radio stations. She loved having her own talk show, and was passionate about her job, deriving great satisfaction and pride from it.

Gabby started dating one of her radio station coworkers, Boris, a very intelligent young man with a great sense of humor. He was able to make her laugh even in the most difficult situations. However, she knew she was not in love with him. Gabby decided to be honest with Boris from the beginning. She explained about her failed relationship to Aaron when she was younger, and Boris was very understanding. He was an interesting and charming companion, as well as a good friend. They built an enjoyable relationship, based on mutual appreciation and respect, that lasted for a few years.

Boris and Gabby traveled a great deal together inside Bulgaria, as well as abroad. With him she felt she could be herself; it was easy to be around him, contrasted with her memory of how difficult it was for her to be with Aaron. Gabby wished that she could love Boris and could be able to marry him. His parents adored her! But if she had married him, it would have been for very selfish reasons. To have someone around whom she does not love, but out of convenience; this was not fair to Boris. She was mature enough to understand that she needed to let him go; he deserved to find someone who would truly love him. Gabby was longing for the passionate love she had once experienced with Aaron.

Emma had not given up on the idea of bringing Gabby to the United States. In her typical persuasive way, she convinced Gabby to play the green card lottery a few times. The last time Emma even took upon herself the task of sending the letter from the USA, since someone told her that would increase the chances of winning. Gabby went along with this plan just to satisfy her friend.

To Gabby's surprise, after a few years of unsuccessfully trying the lottery, she finally won. Emma was ecstatic from joy; Gabby, not so much. By following closely Emma's story of moving to a foreign country, she knew how difficult new beginnings could be. On her radio show, she was currently featuring stories of Bulgarians who had emigrated abroad. She had learned that, even with enough funds and the support of family and friends, people often cannot adjust to the unfamiliar demands of living in a foreign country. Her own parents' history of living for a year in East Germany made her cautious about making such an important decision. She had not made up her mind yet, and had heard stories of people who get their green cards and then travel back and forth between two countries. Gabby thought that might be a good possibility for her.

Since she had one year to prepare all her papers, pass an interview and get a visa, Gabby was not in a hurry to make her final decision. Then, a couple of important events happened in her life that tilted the scale.

First, at the radio station where she was working, there were unexpected changes. The ownership of the broadcast changed. Some of the co-workers she had built meaningful relationships with had left, due to the new bosses' very different visions about how to run the programs. New people were nominated for important positions at the station. They did not have the required qualifications, but they did have good relationships with the owners. Gabby's forthright nature could not agree with such methods of conducting business. So, she voiced her disagreement and was told that if she did not like how the business was run now, she could leave. So, Gabby happily and quickly left the radio station, even though she regretted ending her beloved show, which was her identity, since she had built it from scratch.

Second, her parents' restaurant was not as profitable as it had been in the beginning. Rose and Miho had made some questionable financial decisions that would affect not only the business, but the future of the entire family. Since Gabby had lots of free time now, she was helping out in the restaurant. This was certainly not what she had dreamt about or studied for, but it gave her the valuable experience of working in a completely different area of life. She was mentally preparing herself for the emigration procedure, and for life abroad. The only pleasant event during this time of Gabby's life was the upcoming wedding of her best friend Emma.

7

The Wedding

"Pine tree is bending forward in pain.
A young maiden is letting go of her family.

Forgive me, my big family, and you, my birth mother,
Who has carried me for 9 months in her heart,
For 9 months in her heart, and for 3 years in her arms.

I am now leaving you, to my younger sisters.

To my younger sisters, to my unmarried brothers."

    – A traditional Bulgarian folk wedding song, played at
    the moment when the bride leaves her father's house to
    live with her husband's family.

After living for so many years abroad, Emma and Angel, her husband-to-be, were blessed with the opportunity to come back and get married in their Motherland. The wedding day was set for the middle of July. A summer wedding was something Emma had envisioned since she was a little girl.

In the recent Communist past, only civil unions were allowed in Bulgaria. The identical marriage ceremony for the entire country at that time had been approved by the government and was performed only at city halls. The event was dull, boring, and outdated. People were not able to get married in church or in any other religious places at that time. Emma and Angel were lucky that, when they decided to tie the knot, young people had options. They were finally free to choose what they wanted to happen at the weddings, without being managed by their parents, or by the government. In the country, a shortage of goods no longer existed, either. Weddings could be as lavish and flamboyant as the families could afford. More recently, young people had in fact started to return to traditional weddings.

So, the young couple opted for a mix of an old-fashioned marriage ceremony with some modern twists. The bride and groom would be dressed in traditional Bulgarian folk costumes. The couple did not want a church wedding, despite their parents' preference. The wedding would take place outdoors, at one of the fashionable, newly built outdoor gardens. The reception would be held at a restaurant that served traditional Bulgarian food.

Emma decided to hire a wedding planner, as was the custom in the USA, although uncommon in her native country. Despite being satisfied by the expertise of the wedding planner, she still needed Gabby's help and opinions. This was an enjoyable time for both friends. They were slowly getting used to each other again, and so were reviving their previous closeness. They were able to effectively coordinate their plans, not only for the wedding, but also for Gabby's upcoming trip to the United States. Following the wedding, the newly married couple would be traveling to Italy for their several-week honeymoon. After that, they will go back to the States to await Gabby's arrival.

The wedding was planned for a Sunday, as was customary. The weather was perfect for a summer wedding, as Emma had hoped. The events during this fateful day begin in mid-morning, when Angel went to the house of their "kumove"—roles similar to the best man—"kum"—and the maid of honor—"kuma" The kumove was an older married couple who would guide the newlyweds in their family life; and would be baptizing the young couple's future children as well. After that, the groom, with "kumove" and other friends, headed to Emma's parents' house, riding in a cavalcade of cars, motorcycles and a limousine for the bride, all attractively decorated with flowers and balloons.

They were all preparing to symbolically "buy" the bride from her family. Emma was hiding in her childhood room, fully dressed in traditional white-and-red wedding attire, waiting for the groom's party to arrive. Family members, plus Gabby and a couple of other close girlfriends, were also guarding her. When the clamorous party arrived, Gabby took off one of the bride's elegant shoes, and gave it to the groom so he could fill it with money. The shoe was returned to him a few times, as the family pretended that the money was not enough to pay for such a beautiful bride as Emma to be given away. This custom was accompanied by traditional songs, folk music played by the orchestra, and lots of laughter.

After the bride and the groom were finally reunited, the couple and their parents and the whole party danced the "horo" (a famous Bulgarian folk dance) in front of the building. It was led by the "kum"—the most important person at the wedding—after the bride and groom, of course. All the neighbors (and even passers-by) were welcomed to join them during the dancing. A specially hired video photographer followed the happy couple and their guests around for the entire day, so that all important moments of the wedding were properly documented.

The actual wedding ceremony was performed outside in the garden, under an intricate arch covered with flowers. Unlike typical American weddings, the ceremony was officiated not by a minister or a notary, but by a civil clerk. At the beginning of the ceremony, the female clerk recited a heartwarming love poem. The formalities did not take a long time. The clerk asked the bride and the groom if they wanted to get married. After both of them said affirmative answers, they signed the official protocol. Later, they accepted wedding bands, and the groom kissed the bride.

Following the ceremony, all the guests socialized at the garden, drinking champagne and congratulating the newly wedded couple. Emma was shining in her splendor as being the most exquisite bride. She was so happy and very pleased to be the center of attention—after all, she was a singer and an actress. Being the center of attention was her domain. Angel was making lots of jokes with the guests. He seemed to be very happy and relaxed during the entire wedding and afterwards at the party.

When the newly wedded couple entered the restaurant, Emma's mother-in-law welcomed them with a loaf of beautifully decorated circular ritual bread. She broke the bread into pieces and fed both bride and groom. One piece of bread was dipped in salt, and the other in honey. This part of the tradition represented the happy and the difficult moments the couple would inevitably endure during their marriage. On the dance floor, there was a white piece of fabric, decorated with flowers. The couple was supposed to walk through it and dance over the fabric.

The first dance by the newly wedded couple was touching. Both of their mothers had tears in their eyes at that point. After that, the parents of the bride and the groom were called onto the dance floor. Emma danced with her father-in-law; and Angel danced with his mother-in-law. Angel was a good dancer! He had the time of his life dancing classical dances with Emma, and later on, traditional Bulgarian wedding dances with his male friends.

The DJ (Disc Jockey) Emma had invited to work at the wedding came highly recommended. His repertoire included not only traditional Bulgarian folk music, but modern songs as well. The high point of the event was when Emma sang a couple of songs, both in Bulgarian and in English. Every last one of the guests was fascinated by her dulcet voice. The party in general was a great success. Guests would be talking about their memories from the party for years to come.

Some Western traditions, such as throwing the bouquet, were skipped during the wedding; other traditions, like cutting the wedding cake, were preserved. The cake itself was slightly different from typical American wedding cakes: smaller, with only three tiers, decorated with figs and real flowers. No figures of the bride and groom on top of the cake. All the guests enjoyed this most delicious cake.

Another ritual bread had to be broken, this time by the bride and groom themselves. Facing each other, they held the bread over their heads. The meaning of this tradition was that whoever breaks the biggest part of the bread will take the lead in the new family. It was no surprise that the bigger piece of the bread was now in Emma's hands!

Gabby was dressed in a beautiful red silk dress decorated with dark blue roses, and wildflowers in her hair that matched Emma's wedding bouquet. She fully enjoyed herself during her friend's big day—dancing, laughing, eating delicious bread and cake. Her heart felt warmed by the music, the dancing, the traditions that people cherish. Gabby's soul was overflowing with love and hopes for the future of her newly married friends; and for her own future as well.

Part IV

1

Emigrating to the USA

"And the danger is that in this move toward new horizons and far directions, that I may lose what I have now, and not find anything except loneliness."

– Sylvia Plath, (1932–1963), an American poet, novelist, and short-story writer. She was awarded a Pulitzer Prize in Poetry in 1982, posthumously.

I wonder how my Mom felt when she was leaving our country many years ago, Gabby thought when she was in her seat in the flight to New York. It had been almost month and a half since Emma's and Angel's wedding. The newlyweds were waiting for Gabby's arrival with bated breath.

Gabby did not want either her parents or her sisters to come to the airport. So she said goodbye to them at home. It was better that way. No tears, no last-minute kisses and hugs at the gate. That scenario would have broken her heart.

She needed her head to be clear, her emotions to be under control; she needed to focus on the experience itself. This was her first transatlantic flight; and her first time leaving her native country, not to go on vacation, but actually to live somewhere else. She was frightened and excited at once, like the first time she made love. Gabby smiled to herself. How long ago was that? And where is Aaron now? Maybe fate will bring them together again.

Zoe the cat was in a cage at the luggage section of the aircraft. Gabby had given the cat a light sedative so she could tolerate the flight easily.

Gabby had taken two connecting flights prior to this one. Tired from the uncomfortable seats and from the long, exhausting wait at the airport, the young woman was lucky that, on this flight, nobody was seated next to her. That meant more room for her tired legs; plus, she would not be forced to talk to someone. She put on her headphones and turned on classical music, which was usually able to relax her. More often than not, she could sleep in any type of moving object—a car, a train, an airplane. So, she was hoping that she would fall asleep soon and sleep during the entire flight. She knew that flight attendants usually do not wake up passengers; they just leave their food on the little tables. Even though Gabby was curious to try the different types of food she would eat later, now she just needed to rest.

She had no experience of traveling in such a big aircraft. There were probably 200 people packed in tightly. The buzz coming from both the motors and the conversation of the passengers was almost unbearable. Gabby was pondering the future. What will it bring her? Was she going to be able to adjust to life in the new country? Would she find a good job?

She was concerned that the level of her knowledge of English was not good enough to get her the job she wants. But she was prepared to start with any job she could find.

Gabby left her country with a limited amount of funds; also, she will need to put aside some money to be sent to her parents every month, because they needed her help. Millions of Bulgarians were in the same position at that time because the Bulgarian economy was not improving at the desired speed. Numerous young people were leaving the country in search of better job opportunities, in order to be able to support themselves, their families, and their parents.

Gabby was one of the lucky one; she was going to a place where she has friends who will support her at the beginning. But she could not rely on Emma and Angel for everything. They have their jobs, their careers; they just got married and bought a new house and will probably start a family soon. Gabby sighed and closed her eyes. She placed her fears and uncertainties on the side for now and tried to take a nap. "I hope I will wake up on time to see New York City from the airplane window!"

"Miss?" the flight attendant softly addressed Gabby, who opened her eyes. "We are approaching New York." Gabby thanked him, lifted the window shade and was astonished by the breathtaking panoramic view of the skyscrapers below. She had never seen such tall buildings in her life! In the past, she had seen some pictures of New York, but nothing could compare to this real bird's-eye view. That day, the sky was colored in iridescent, vividly blue colors. There was not even one cloud in the sky; and because the summer sun was glowing brightly, that made the scenery even more extraordinary.

It was mid-afternoon when Gabby arrived at the Big Apple; then it took a few hours to go through Customs and Immigration. She had to stand in a long line with all her luggage and the cat, Zoe, in a cage. Gabby started to worry that her friends were going to spend hours at the airport waiting for her. She did not know that they were actually stuck in traffic, worried about her.

Finally, the Immigration officer gave Gabby back all her paperwork. She was free to go! So, she looked around and found a pay phone. (Emma had been smart enough to give Gabby some spare change when they were together in Bulgaria.) Gabby was delighted to hear Emma's sweet voice on the line, as it reminded her that she was not alone in this big new city. Gabby assured her friend that she did not mind waiting for them. What other choice did she have, after all?! She did not know anyone else in this entire city.

She sat on the nearby bench and immersed herself in observation of the passing crowds. What a conglomerate of humans, and so many of them! People from all races and nationalities, dressed in every possible way—from business attire and elegant clothes to mismatched street clothing and run-down shoes. She could hear passengers speaking so many different languages. Even the English that she studied in the past from British books sounded so different here. How would she survive in this modern Babylon? Gabby did not know this yet but observing New Yorkers and taking their photos would become her favorite pastime for the next few years.

From a distance, she saw Emma's slender figure and beautiful, long, blond hair. She waved enthusiastically at her friend, and saw Angel, just moseying along. She likes how he walks in a leisurely manner; he and Emma look so good together! She was so happy to hug them both tightly. Zoe the cat was ecstatic at finally being reunited with her owner. It seems that she does remember Emma well after so many years of separation! Angel took the cart with Gabby's luggage on it, like a good gentleman does; and they all strolled out toward the parking lot.

Gabby's face was glued to the window of the minivan her friend was driving. She was like a child in a toy store; all was new and exciting to her. Everything looks different here—the cars, the traffic lights, the pedestrians, the uncommon-looking buildings. Traffic was unbelievably busy. Gabby had never seen such heavy traffic. Some of the buildings they passed were gray, grimy, scary-looking. Many of the pedestrians looked like lost souls.

Emma was driving like a lunatic. "Does she always drive like this?" Gabby asked Angel.

"You have no idea!" he laughed. They were in the car for one hour until they finally reached her friend's house. Gabby liked the streets of their neighborhood at once; they looked clean, well-landscaped and well-organized. The atmosphere was very different here, compared to the streets they had passed as they drove away from the airport. The houses all look alike —two-story buildings, all with garages and identical driveways. Each house had a small garden in the back and a little patch of grass in the front.

When the young people entered the house, Emma showed Gabby a small in-law addition to the main house in the backyard, saying, "Here is your new home, my dear friend!" Gabby liked her new place right away. Angel dragged her luggage in and left it in the tiny living room. Emma had placed flowers in multiple vases around the house. When Gabby opened the bedroom door, she saw a little basket with tokens on the bed and a folded towel, like in fine hotel rooms. Gabby turned to her friend and hugged and kissed her. She forgot how exciting and interesting life could be around Emma.

Zoe liked the yard. Although she was raised as an indoor cat in an apartment, suddenly she had an entire two-story house and a yard to herself. Although she was an older cat now, she was still very active and fun to be around. So, for now, everyone was pleased with the living arrangements.

Emma and Angel prepared a whole fiesta, with Gabby's favorite dishes. The three of them sat at the outdoor chairs and table in the yard; they ate, they drank some wine, they talked, and they laughed. Gabby was surprised to hear the song of crickets in the yard. So, they have crickets here, too! She looked up at the sky. The constellations looked different than the ones she was used to seeing in the night's sky in Bulgaria. *I am on the other side of the world now,* she thought to herself, quietly finishing her glass of wine.

The first day of Gabby's new life was coming to an end. She was exhausted, but not able to fall asleep right away, due to the time difference. She was playing again in her head all the events, from the moment she left her hometown to the time she put her head on the pillow here in New York. Tomorrow she will need to call her parents to assure them that she is doing well. "Good night, New York!" she called out softly.

2

The First Day of Her New Life

"Great things are not done by impulse, but by a series of small things brought together."

– George Eliot (1819–1880), English novelist, poet, journalist and a leading writer of the Victorian era. Mary Ann Evans was known by her pen name, George Eliot. She wrote seven novels, set in the English countryside. Her novels are known for their realism, psychological insight, sense of place and detailed depiction of the countryside.

When Gabby woke up the next morning, initially she was a little disoriented. This was not her bed, and this was not her room. After trying slowly to separate her mind from her dreams, she realized she was in her friend Emma's house in the USA, in New York. She smiled. Her new life starts today!

Emma let her friend sleep in. She knew Gabby would need a few days to adjust to the time change, and to the new world around her. Emma took the whole week off work to be able to help Gabby with her adaptation. Today she planned to drive her around, show her where the train station is, and where the stores are around the neighborhood.

But the first thing she needed to do was help her friend unpack. Gabby was famous for her tidiness, and Emma knew that her friend would not start anything important if her room was a mess. Since Emma is a wife now, and her husband is more orderly than she is, she needs to be working on her own organizational skills as well. What better time to start than today?

Emma entered Gabby's living room holding a cup of coffee in each hand. Her calico cat Zoe, who was sleeping on the couch, woke up, gave an absent look to her owner, adjusted her sleeping position, and went right back to snoozing. *Even the cat needs acclimatization!* Emma thought to herself. "Gabby, where are you?" Gabby was in the bedroom, already unpacking and organizing her clothes in the closet. "What an unusual wardrobe section is this!" Gabby observed, pointing at the closet. "Everything is unusual around here, Emma. Do you know that I had difficulty figuring out how to turn on the faucet in the shower?" Gabby laughed, with her unforgettable laugh. Emma knew; she remembered her own first days in the US when she thought she had broken the toilet because the water level was different than in Bulgaria! "Yes, Gabby, here everything is different. It is not like in Europe; here all is new, unusual, bigger, louder, but you will get used to it, and you will love it!" Emma smiled at her friend reassuringly.

"Are you still keeping this old figurine?!" Emma picked up the red, white and blue porcelain doll from the nightstand. Gabby took the toy very carefully from her friend's hands.

"Emma, you know how attached I am to this doll. I took her on all my vacations and little trips. Do you think that I would leave her behind when I crossed the big ocean?!"

Emma just shook her head in disbelief. "C'mon, Gabby, take a shower and get dressed. I have lots of things planned for us to do today!"

At this time in their life as a newly wedded couple, Emma was the planner and the executor of most of the family's daily activities. Since Angel was studying diligently in order to pass his bar exam, he has a study room set up on the second floor of their home. Emma wanted to spend more time outside the house with Gabby so that Angel could have peace and quiet to study.

She wanted to take Gabby to see Manhattan now, but probably they would wait and go on the weekend, with Angel. Emma had lots of activities planned, but she did not want to overwhelm her friend in the beginning. Even Emma, with her endless energy and her extroverted nature, had had a difficult time adjusting to life in the USA. She read an article recently about the culture shock people encounter in a different country. Now, looking back at her own experiences in America, she realized that she did in fact suffer from initial culture shock. The condition was not recognized by either Emma or Angel at that time. Emma was trying to prevent Gabby from facing the same difficulties.

Later that day, when the two girlfriends were alone in the car, Emma showed Gabby the list she had made of all the important places, numbers, and emergency contacts in her life.

"It is difficult for me to believe that you are becoming this organized person, Emma!" Gabby teased her.

"You have to be organized and disciplined if you want to achieve something in this country!"

"I think married life suits you well, Emma." But Emma just smirked at that remark.

Emma continued reading the to-do list she had created for Gabby: going to the Social Security office; getting a cell phone; filling out applications for jobs. "Gabby, are you listening to me?"

"Yes, Emma, I am listening—and I am trying to memorize my way back home at the same time!" For now, Gabby was going to ride a bike through the neighborhood over to the train station, if she needed to go to the city. Later, when she has saved some money for a car, her friends will get her a used one. Emma would still drive her now and then, when she is available. One aspect of Emma's job was to sing at different city events, and she drove long distances on a daily basis. So...Gabby needed to become self-reliant in a short time.

"I would prefer you start working somewhere where you will speak with Americans mostly," Emma observed. "On the other hand, there is a Bulgarian restaurant in the city. You do know the restaurant business, in fact, and it should be easy for you to get, as a starter job. But...you would not be able to practice English much there. Which do you think would be the better choice?"

"I think a job at the restaurant would be a good beginning. Maybe later on, I could apply for a job at a newspaper," Gabby answered confidently.

"I need to sign you up for English school for adults," Emma observed. You will meet people from all over the world there. You could make some friends; plus, you will get used to the different ways in which people speak English. You could take some computer classes there as well; but the schools are closed now until September. Besides, you need to get your SSI number first." Emma was thinking aloud.

"I need to get my what?!" Gabby asked as she raised her eyebrows.

Emma laughed. "SSI. Social Security Identification. Yes, you will get used to using abbreviations, my friend. Americans use them a lot."

The two friends had fun grocery shopping together. Well, actually mostly Emma, who was teasing and laughing at her girlfriend's amusement with every new detail in the store, was having fun. Gabby insisted on paying cash for everything, while Emma wanted to teach her about the convenience of using debit and credit cards. "We need to go to the bank now and open an account for you. You cannot walk around in New York carrying lots of cash, Gabby!"

When they got home, Gabby offered to cook for her friends. But Emma chuckled, "I am the chef, Gabby. Did you forget that? I will give you the pleasure of loading the dishwasher," Emma chuckled. Gabby had never operated such a modern machine before, even though at her parents' restaurant they had one outdated commercial dishwasher. So many new things, both trivial and important, she needs to learn in order to adapt to life in a foreign country!

Emma sent her exhausted friend to her little in-law addition in the backyard, so Gabby could take a nice, long nap. *"My first day on American soil is almost over, and I haven't done anything significant yet,"* Gabby brooded while cuddling with Zoe in the bed.

❦ 3 ❧

Gabby in the Big Apple

"What's the use of a great city having temptations if
fellows don't yield to them?"

– P. G. Wodehouse (1881–1975), British author and one
of the most widely read humorists of the 20th century.

In the few weeks that had passed since Gabby's arrival, she
was slowly getting acclimated to the modern and dynamic
life in one of the most influential American cities. The young
Bulgarian was constantly learning new things, having brand-new
experiences, meeting fascinating people. The journalist in her
was very much alive, curious, and thriving. She was constantly
taking notes about all the interesting events, places and people.
She, Emma and Angel cruised through Manhattan a few times
as Gabby took many photos with Emma's professional camera.
She liked some parts of the city much more than others, and
especially enjoyed the town at night-time and all the alluring
neon lights; she marveled at the glow of the iconic Times Square
billboards and at the famous Empire State Building.

Gabby and Emma took a few long walks in Central Park. They even had a delicious improvised picnic one day at the park. This place reminded Gabby of the Sea Garden in her hometown. She liked the horse-drawn carriages they saw at one of the entrances to the park. She wished one day she would be taking a ride with someone she loves in one of those carriages. Gabby was emailing many photos to her family, keeping in touch with them on a daily basis.

What she could not capture in those photos, however, was the smell of the city. During her trips through European cities in the past, she had discovered that each city had its own unique odor. To her, New York could be recognized by pizza cooking, or by the mouth-watering aroma of fresh-baked bagels. Sometimes the city smelled clean and fresh; at other times, the stench from the garbage cans on the streets was unbearable.

The buzz of the big-city traffic did not bother her. It was more unusual, and exhausting, to get used to the bustling crowds on the streets. Gabby liked to visit museums and art galleries, especially in the mornings on workdays, when few people are visiting. She would love to attend interesting theatrical plays one day. For now, Gabby sensed that her current level of colloquial English would not allow full enjoyment of the actors. Emma promised to take her to see a Broadway show when the season started in the fall. This time of Gabby's life, when she was exploring the new city on her own, reminded her of her early college years in the Capital of Bulgaria. As it was in the past, one of the most enjoyable times for her was roaming the obscure old streets of New York; finding—unexpectedly—some unknown (to her) historic building; or a hidden coffee shop or bookstore. This was difficult to describe to someone who has not experienced the blend of modern and ancient in New York.

The schools are not open yet, but Gabby was following Emma's advice to watch TV shows and listen to the TV news when possible. To Emma, this was a proven way of learning a foreign language—not from books, but from listening to conversations between real people. Emma encouraged her friend to speak with strangers; to order restaurant food on the phone or when she dined out. Gabby's English language skills were definitely improving; she was slowly becoming more confident and secure. Her transition to her new life was surely not easy, but it was happening, and it was rewarding.

Gabby started a job at the Bulgarian restaurant in the city. As expected, it did not pay very well, but it provided her with much-needed income. And she was able to send some of her hard-earned money to her family in Bulgaria. To get to work, she usually drove her bike to the train station and then caught a train. She had already been on the subway, and she rode the Staten Island ferry a few times. She was gradually becoming a true New Yorker!

During her days off, Emma took Gabby on road trips outside the city. They visited the neighboring states of New Jersey and Connecticut, and fell in love with some of the small idyllic towns they discovered during those trips. This pastoral atmosphere reminded Gabby of the countryside of her native country. Both women relished this time together, when they could get away from the demands of life in the Big City. They talked about their shared memories and their future plans. The weather was still summery warm, but fall was arriving with its special features: colder mornings; the slowly-changing colors of the leaves to orange and red; the big flocks of different birds—from ospreys to geese and hummingbirds gathering together to migrate south. In Bulgaria, this time of the fall, or autumn, was called "Gypsy's summer." It was interesting for Gabby to learn that in the United States, the name for this time of year was "Indian summer." This was one of the many fascinating similarities between the two seemingly separate languages and cultures that Gabby discovered constantly.

The English school for adults added to Gabby's confidence with the language, just as Emma had predicted. Gabriella was attending classes there in the mornings and working at the Bulgarian restaurant in the evenings. At the school, Gabby met fascinating people from all over the world, from different backgrounds, who were studying English. Gabby was easy to talk to, and everyone was willing to share their life stories with her. Since Gabby's journalist's notebook was always close by, she accrued material for many articles and books. If only she could write them in excellent English!

Gabby had always been fascinated by people's stories. That was the reason she started the radio talk show in her hometown. Now, she was making wonderful friends at the school in New York. Studying and working were the activities that kept her busy; they gave her life a meaningful purpose during this beginning time in New York.

On this warm September Tuesday morning, Gabby was in her class, as usual. The group of adults had just started sharing and correcting their homework assignment. Unexpectedly, the teacher was called to the school Principal's office. Students gave each other puzzled looks. They sensed that something unusual had just happened. The atmosphere in the room changed. Students from other classes were gathering in the cafeteria, where the TV was on. Even with their limited understanding of English, Gabby and her classmates were able to comprehend that the World Trade Center had just been attacked by terrorists who hijacked airplanes. They watched in horror images of the burning Twin Tower buildings and workers racing away from the inferno. The voice of the Principal over the Public Address system was trembling when he told students to go home immediately, and to be safe.

Gabby was still in shock when her cell phone rang. Emma was coming immediately to pick her up. For a while, Gabby waited on the street with some of her classmates. People were apprehensive and fearful. Nobody had a clear idea about what was happening, and why. For them, as foreigners, it was even more difficult to comprehend the magnitude of the situation. The whole event was surreal. Later, when she was in the car with Emma, they listened to the radio. Emma translated some of the information to her. "Maybe we need to go somewhere to donate blood, since many people were injured," Gabby suggested. "I will make some inquiring calls about that now," Emma reassured her. This tragic event reminded Gabby about some of the movies she had watched as a child, back in Bulgaria, about World War II. She had never imagined there would be a likelihood for something like this to happen in real life, and in the United States!

The sensation of something unreal having happened continued for many weeks. Those videos of the burning buildings and workers jumping to their deaths from high windows were played on television multiple times. Americans were very scared for their safety and security, and for the future of their country. Everyone had to learn right away how to be aware of their surroundings. Gabby was more careful now when she rode the train, or the subway, or when she roamed the streets of New York, the city she was just starting to love, alone.

All schools in the United States were closed for about a week, out of caution. After they finally opened again, many changes were implemented. Security was enhanced at schools, as well as at the entrances to all governmental, and some public, buildings. Security at the airports was increased significantly. Many restrictions about bringing on certain items during flights were implemented. Gabby and Emma learned about those restrictions first-hand when they flew to Bulgaria the next time, on summer vacation. Life as people had known it had changed forever.

Emma's and Gabby's relatives and friends from all over the world were constantly calling them during those initial weeks after September 11th. They wanted to check to see if the two women had been affected by the horrific events. Some suggested that Emma and Gabby come back home to live in Bulgaria. It was impossible to predict what the future would bring. For now, independently of each other, they each decided to continue building their lives in their new adopted country, despite the horror of the Twin Towers disaster.

4

Holidays

"Call it a clan, call it a network, call it a tribe,
call it a family: whatever you call it, whoever you are,
you need one."

> – Jane Howard (1935-1996), American journalist, author,
> and educator. Jane Howard worked at *Life* magazine
> from 1956 to 1972, contributed articles to many
> publications and wrote several books; most well-known
> was her biography of Margaret Mead.

Emma and Angel were Gabby's family now. They helped her with the adaptation to America, as it was customary for Bulgarians to help their friends and family under any circumstances whatsoever. Gabby was mostly interacting with Emma, since her job was freelance. Angel was busy, working long fixed hours at a famous law firm after he had successfully passed his exam. All three usually spent time together on weekends. They did grocery shopping and cooking together; went to movies; took long walks; and explored the city for new restaurants and interesting places.

For Gabby, it was comfortable to be with both. They never made her feel like she was the fifth wheel. Emma and Gabby had been very close for many years, but Gabby grew to accept Angel into their tight circle of friends. She liked his spontaneity, his mischievous sense of humor, his intelligence and his ambition. In him, she finally found the big brother she never had.

Her first American Thanksgiving was a new, very enjoyable time in her life for Gabby. She had learned a great deal about the history behind the holiday at the English school. One night, the three friends watched a captivating movie about the upcoming holiday. Gabby had discovered that she enjoyed watching movies and shows better now, because her knowledge of the English language had increased. Emma and Angel did not have a housewarming party when they bought their house, due to the wedding. So, they decided to make this Thanksgiving especially festive—not only for Gabby, but for themselves as well. It was not only Gabby's first Thanksgiving, but also their first Thanksgiving in the new house.

The young couple invited a few of their coworkers to celebrate with them, since they did not have family around. Emma offered that Gabby could invite some friends from her work and from her school if she wished. So, there was an interesting mix of Americans, Bulgarians, Hispanics and a few other Eastern Europeans attending the gathering. This was a true example of the melting pot United States was known for.

Emma decided to cook all the traditional American dishes for the holiday's festive lunch. And Gabby greatly enjoyed eating them all. She had not eaten turkey since her early years in her grandmother's house; turkey was not a common poultry in

Bulgaria. Most of Emma's and Angel's guests watched sports on television, as that was customary for the holiday. Only Emma and Gabby watched the traditional Macy's Thanksgiving Day Parade on television; Gabby was as fascinated as a child. She promised herself that one day she would be watching it live, as a member of the crowd on the streets.

It was the Friday before the Christmas break. Friday was Gabby's favorite day of the week now. Besides being payday, Fridays were so-called "socializing days" at school. Usually on Fridays, students collected money and bought pizzas for everyone. Other times, their teacher brought them doughnuts or bagels for breakfast. Once a month, students brought home-cooked traditional dishes from their native country to share with their peers at school. Along with a presentation of their culture and history, this event was very educational.

Today was Gabby's turn to bring food and to present facts about Bulgaria. Emma and Gabby made the famous pastry, banitcha, with phyllo dough and feta cheese. Both of them stayed up until late at night to fill the trays with the delicious golden baked dough. The dish was liked by everyone, and so was Gabby's presentation. She put some traditional Bulgarian folk music on the computer for her classmates to listen to. Hearing the familiar rhythms brought tears to her eyes. Would she be able to visit her homeland soon?

Gabby fell in love with the Christmassy decorations in New York City. She had always loved the winter and the snow but celebrating this season in the big city provided her with endless reasons for joy. She had never seen so many elegant decorations on every public or private building before. Gabby likes all the wreaths on the front doors; and she enjoys observing the colorfully decorated Christmas trees set up in the front windows of houses and apartments.

Emma and Gabby attended the famous ceremony, the lighting of the huge Christmas tree at Rockefeller Center. The atmosphere was exhilarating. Gabby was amazed to see so many adults there—smiling, singing, cheering like children when the twinkling lights came on. This brought back treasured memories of the first time she saw a decorated tree as a child. Her grandfather Ivan usually went to the forest and cut the Christmas tree for the family every year. After the Christmas tree was set in the living room, Gabby and her sisters decorated the tree with mostly home-made ornaments. They did not have lights on the tree; instead they used tinsel to add some sparkle, and cotton balls to imitate snow. Even this simply decorated tree had brought enormous joy to their lives at the time.

Gabby loves coming to Manhattan, an adventure that does not happen often. She especially enjoys walking through the alley with the international flags flying. Emma and she invented a little game in which they test each other's knowledge about various countries' flags. Each time she sees the Bulgarian flag waving in the wind, her heart beats faster. In December, along with other festive activities, Gabby and Emma found time to go ice skating. This was Gabby's first time on the ice rink. With the exception of a couple of minor falls on the ground, accompanied by lots of laughs and jokes, the skating went very well.

The merriment of the season continued at Emma's house. This was one of the busiest times of the year for Emma's business, but she found the time to fully participate in all the traditional activities. The three friends embellished the house, inside and out. The women spent lots of time shopping for gifts for everyone, including Zoe the cat. The idea of piling up so many wrapped gifts under the tree was very unusual for Gabby. In her native country, she usually got and gave only one present, usually a book. *Her friends had become Americanized*, she thought to herself, looking at the pyramid of presents under the tree in Emma's house.

On Christmas Eve, all three friends were free from work; even Angel came home unusually early. After a light dinner, they spent the evening in front of the fireplace, drinking eggnog, talking, and watching seasonal movies. The atmosphere was homey and festive at the same time. The next morning was the first time Gabby spent half a day in her pajamas, opening presents. Emma took lots of funny photos of the three of them that morning. Gabby went for a long walk around the neighborhood. She loves walking in the cold air, looking at the decorated houses. The holiday dinner was traditional, but they did not invite any guests this time. Emma was still recovering from all the Thanksgiving cooking and entertaining.

New Year's Eve and New Year's Day are usually huge celebrations in Bulgaria. People traditionally dine out at fine restaurants, where they are entertained by popular artists, or host parties at their homes. Gabby decided to invite her friends to the restaurant where she was working that night. That way, they could add a modern spin to old traditions. This was one of the downfalls of being a hospitality worker—working during holidays. After Gabby's shift ended, long after midnight, all three of them roamed the festive streets of New York. The crisp air was filled with music and good cheer. People were dancing in the streets; the three amigos joined them, dancing, laughing, having a great time.

Emma did not risk singing outside in the cold, however, as she needed to take good care of her voice. She was dreaming big, that one day she would be at Time Square, singing and performing during a New Year's Eve show. Gabby's wish for the New Year was to finally find her true love. Angel wished for a baby; Emma just laughed and hugged him. The friends got home in the early morning hours—absolutely exhausted, but happy. What would the New Year bring them?

Gabby was a little concerned that her friends, a newly married couple, were not spending enough alone time together. Emma usually laughed when her friend shared those concerns with her. After the first unforgettable Christmas and New Year's celebrations together, Emma wanted all of them to go on a ski trip in the mountains of Colorado. This time, Gabby had to put her foot down and insist that Emma and Angel take a little vacation by themselves. They needed time alone as a couple. She also felt that her friends had already spent enough money on her during the Christmas season. A ski trip was a luxury she could not afford on a part-time salary. Plus, she did not want Emma to pay for her accommodations, in addition to all the other presents she had already received.

Gabby decided that she would stay home with Zoe the cat. Her winter break from school was over, so she would go back to her routine of working and going to school. Emma was torn between the desire to spend time alone with her husband and leaving her friend to fend for herself. Nevertheless, Emma and Angel left in the middle of the second week of January. They were supposed to come back that Sunday.

On Saturday afternoon, Gabby was tucked under her blanket, with Zoe peacefully sleeping on her chest. The wind outside was blowing fiercely. She had heard on the news that a storm was expected on Sunday, and was concerned about her friends' flight tomorrow. To soothe her mind, she put a romantic comedy on TV. Gabby liked having the house to herself for a few days. It felt like the time in Sofia, when she was alone with Zoe in Emma's apartment.

Her thoughts were startled by the phone ringing. Emma's voice was unrecognizable on the wire. "Emma, slow down, please! I don't understand what you are saying!" After her friend calmed down, she explained that Angel had broken his leg while skiing. They would be away for a few more days because he needed to be transported to the nearest town for surgery at a hospital. The surgeon would put some pins in the leg so it could heal properly. Gabby hung up with a heavy feeling in her heart.

No, she did not mind being alone for a few more days. Rather, the heaviness came from feeling guilty about not going with her friends on this trip. Of course, she knew that her thinking was irrational. How could she have prevented this incident from happening? Still, the feeling of guilt was definitely there.

She remembered very well the time her father broke his leg, a long time ago. He was then off work for a few months. He did not have surgery but needed to have extensive physical therapy. She was guessing that Angel's condition was much worse than that, and so the healing process would take longer. How would this illness affect Angel's job, or Emma's relationship with her husband?

5

An Unexpected Meeting

*"The best parts of any story, to me,
are the unexpected things."*

– Carl Sandburg (1878–1967), Swedish-American poet,
bio-grapher, journalist and editor. He won three
Pulitzer Prizes, two for his poetry and one for his
biography of Abraham Lincoln.

As Gabby suspected, the recovery process for Angel's broken leg took a long time. He was able to do part of his job from home, on his laptop and on his phone. A physical therapist came to their house a few times to assess how safe the home environment was for the recovery process, and to teach the patient how to walk on crutches. She also taught Gabby and Emma how to transfer him to a wheelchair, when they needed to take him for a walk outside. The two women took good care of Angel. His body was young and strong. Still, his fracture was a serious one, and he needed a few months to fully recuperate.

Emma got an offer to sing on a television show, an opportunity she had been waiting for for years. So, Gabby took over most of the responsibilities for Angel and for running the house. The "family" talked together one night and decided that it would be more practical for Gabby to stop working at the restaurant. Angel needed a full-time caregiver for a few months, and they did not want to bring someone from outside the "family" to do that. Gabby was happy to be able to reciprocate at least some of the care and help her friends were constantly giving her. At this time, Gabby left the house only in the mornings, to go to school. Emma spent the mornings with her husband; Angel was Gabby's responsibility in the afternoon.

Angel and Gabby then got very close to each other. It was inevitable, since they spent most of their time together, sharing a great deal of their thoughts and stories. Plus, they had discovered many similarities in their characters, and in their attitudes towards life. They were both quiet introverts, they both liked reading, and for the area around them to be organized. Gabby's favorite pastime for the few months she was Angel's caregiver was taking him for a ride in the wheelchair around the neighborhood.

Gabby was already familiar with her surroundings. Angel had not had much time to walk around his own neighborhood, because he came home late from work. Both discovered that they enjoyed looking at houses; discussing what they liked or did not like about them, and how they would change them.

The cast from Angel's leg was soon removed, and he started going to physical therapy at the Mount Sinai Beth Israel Medical Center twice a week. Emma usually accompanied her husband during those morning appointments. On this cold April morning, however, she needed to be at the TV station; Gabby decided to skip school and help Angel so he would not miss his appointment. Angel allowed Gabby to drive his car until they got to the train station. After that, they took the train to get to the hospital. They were both in a good mood, talking and laughing. Angel was making funny jokes about Gabby's driving this morning. She looked at him and was suddenly smitten by the desire to kiss his lips. She felt scared by her own thoughts, and looked away. Mercifully, their train stop was coming next. She turned toward Angel in an attempt to help him stand up. She felt the heat of his hand against hers and quickly took her hand away. "I can do this by myself, Gabby. I am a strong man," he smiled at her, a spark of amusement in his eyes. *Is he feeling what I am feeling?* Gabby did not want to find out the answer to this question.

The young woman was waiting for Angel outside the hospital, smoking. She had returned to this unhealthy habit from her youth since she moved to the USA, maybe due to the stress of the adaptation. Gabby saw from a distance a familiar dark face. Where did she know this man from? Was it from her English school, or had she seen him at her job? Since she moved to the USA, Gabby had moments of uncertainty when she saw someone for the first time. She often asked herself the same questions—did she know that person from Bulgaria, or from here?

Suddenly her brain was flooded with memories. Aaron?! This is impossible, this man is not him! Her vision was tricking her. This man's head was balding, and he had a mustache. In her memory, one of Aaron's best features was his full head of dark curly hair. Still, the man strongly resembles someone she knew from the past. Aaron's father—that was who she was looking at! He slowed his walk, and their eyes met. Those deep-green eyes were unchanged by time. "Gabby!" She saw the joy on his face, and his big smile. They both looked at each other in utter disbelief—imagine meeting in such a serendipitous way, thousands of miles away from their old country! "How?" "When?" "What are you doing here?" were questions they were asking, then interrupting each other.

At this very moment, Gabby remembered that Angel's appointment was probably over by this time. She asked Aaron if he had time to meet her friend. They both entered the waiting area of the physical therapy part of the hospital. Angel was not surprised to see Gabby walking with a man in a white coat. A surprised look came to his face when the doctor addressed him in Bulgarian. Gabby introduced them. Angel invited Aaron to dinner at his house. "It isn't every day when someone unexpectedly meets an old friend from Bulgaria in New York," he said. Gabby was a little surprised by this turn of events. Angel had been homebound for months, with only the two women around him. He was probably longing for male company. Angel took control of the situation; exchanged phone numbers with Aaron, texted him his address. Before Gabby was able to open her mouth in protest, the dinner date was set, and Aaron was shaking her hand. She was appreciative that he did not kiss her in front of Angel.

During the train ride back home, Gabby was silent. Angel sensed her disapproval and did not initiate conversation. Although they barely looked at each other during the trip, they had discerned what the other person was thinking. Actually,

Gabby did not know what she was supposed to be thinking or feeling at that moment. Her long-buried affections for Aaron had surfaced, unforeseen. She thought those old wounds had healed a long time ago. But now, maybe because of the suddenness of their meeting, or because they met in a foreign country, those feelings had reappeared.

On the other hand, her current affection for Angel was opening up new wounds in her heart. She was not supposed to be falling in love with her best friend's husband. This was so wrong! Gabby felt that she was in a trap. She lives in their house, Emma trusts her. Angel is supposed to be her big brother, her treasured friend. He never showed inappropriate behavior toward her. So why does she feel this way? The young woman sighed.

"Are you thinking about your friend?" Angel asked her half-jokingly.

"Yes, I am," Gabby smiled through her tears. This was safe; thinking about Aaron was safe. Oh, wait, he is married, too. *Well, I do not know his wife, and she is not my best friend!* Gabby was able to find the humor, even in this impossible situation. *I do not even know if he is still married.* Gabby's thought process shifted to a different subject.

"How do you two know each other?" Angel continued with his questions.

"We were lovers, once," Gabby looked straight into his eyes.

"Oh...I am sorry, Gabby, I did not know that. Maybe I should not have invited him for dinner." Gabby assured Angel that she would be happy to see this man, just as an old friend.

When Emma got home that night, Angel shared the experience he and Gabby had today at the hospital. "You met Aaron?! The same one you knew in Bulgaria?" Emma turned toward Gabby.

"Yes, Emma, he is the same one. He had fallen, like thunder from the clear sky" (this was an old Bulgarian saying when something or someone appeared unexpectedly).

"This dinner will be an interesting experience. What should we cook for him? Is he eating kosher only?"

"I don't know, Emma. Not that I remember." What Aaron eats was the last thing on Gabby's mind.

Angel said he wanted moussaka—one of the traditional Bulgarian dishes, with potatoes, ground meat and a sauce on the top. When Emma met Angel, he did not care what he was eating—as long as she cooked it for him. The last few months of staying home had turned her husband into a very picky eater. He would not eat the same dish twice. He even became very particular about where Emma and Gabby shopped for produce.

"I don't know about combining meat and milk in the same dish, Emma." Gabby was thoughtful. Emma responded, "Maybe I will cook one small separate dish for him without the Bechamel sauce. And I will use ground beef or lamb instead of pork. And we will have lots of vegetarian side dishes." Emma was in her element now, planning dinners and parties.

"I will bake some bread!" Gabby had been experimenting with different recipes for bread since she had been off work for a while.

"And I will take care of the liquor bar!" Angel grinned with his big smile, trying to look innocent.

"Maybe he does not drink," Gabby teased him.

"Yeah, he is a Saint! He does not eat non-kosher food, he does not drink, and he definitely does not sleep around when he is engaged," said Emma, who could be very sarcastic.

"I see. Was that what happened to you two?" Gabby sensed a deep tenderness in Angel's question, or perhaps she was imagining something that was not there.

"I am going to bed early tonight. I have a headache starting." Gabby knew that this was a flimsy excuse to make, but she needed to be away from Angel for a few hours.

Lying in her warm bed, hugging her pillow, she was making one impractical plan after another that night. She knew she needed to separate from her friends as soon as possible. But where should she go in this foreign country, with an insufficient amount of money, and without having reliable friends and relatives around? Maybe Aaron was her winning ticket out of all this? Maybe God sent him to her? He was always working in mysterious ways in people's lives.

On the other hand, she remembered her grandmother's saying: "Don't dive into the same water twice." Gabby had already had a painful experience with Aaron. Could she trust him now? Has he changed, has he matured? The dinner was set up for the next day; let us see what the new day will bring her.

Aaron arrived on time and brought a bottle of wine with him; it was the Bulgarian custom to bring food or alcohol when visiting a friend's house. *So, he drinks after all,* Gabby thought. Aaron seems to be impressed by Emma's looks, and by the house, but what was most important, he could not take his eyes off Gabby. He made her feel a bit uncomfortable, so she went to the kitchen and brought the dinner to the dining room. "We did not know what food restrictions you follow, so Emma cooked a separate dish for you." Gabby turned to the man she used to love a decade ago.

"I eat and drink everything." His smile was as charming as she had remembered.

"Tell us your story. How did you end up in the New York hospital?" Angel asked as he poured the famous homemade rakya—a Bulgarian fruit brandy—into Aaron's glass.

"I came to New York a few months ago to work in a special research program. I will be here for 2 years. My family did not come with me; they are back in Israel." *We came to the USA about the same time*, Gabby thought. *Is fate playing with us?* Aaron turned to Gabby: "How did *you* decide to come here?"

"Well, it is a long story," Gabby laughed.

Emma then swirled the conversation toward herself. She started to give a long explanation about how Angel first arrived here; how she herself came as a student; how she tried to convince Gabby for many years to take this decisive step. The dinner was quite pleasant. Aaron tried—and liked—every dish. He gave lots of compliments to Emma for her delicious cooking, and to Gabby for the bread. He was charming and witty, telling amusing stories from his medical practice. He truly resembled his father, not only physically, but also by being an interesting companion. Gabby was observing him closely. She wondered what her life would have been like if they had ended up together.

"How are your parents doing, Aaron?"

"My Mom died last year." Gabby saw tears in his eyes as he said that. She could not say that she was sorry to hear that news, but she felt his pain and had a desire to hug and kiss him at that moment.

The four young people were about the same age and had similar backgrounds. It was easy for them to understand each other. They truly enjoyed themselves that night; maybe the men had a few drinks more than was appropriate, but the atmosphere was heart-to-heart. They danced; they laughed. Emma sang. Everyone was surprised when Aaron took the microphone. His action evoked some treasured memories in Gabby of the times when he played his guitar for her, in bed. She probably had not felt that happy since Emma and Angel's wedding. For the entire dinner, she forgot to think about her strong feelings toward Angel.

"You guys have to come to dinner at my apartment. I am not a good cook, but I can order delicious food from one of the many wonderful restaurants around," Aaron said before he left. It was a custom in Bulgaria for friends to return the visit. Gabby could not help but wonder if this invitation had a hidden meaning.

Gabby and Aaron as Adults

"When love beckons to you, follow him,
Though his ways are hard and steep."

– Kahlil Gibran(1883–1931), Lebanese-American writer, poet and visual artist. Gibran was also considered a philosopher, although he himself rejected the title. He is best known as the author of *The Prophet,* which was first published in the United States in 1923, and has since become one of the best-selling books of all time, having been translated into more than 100 languages.

The sun was gleaming in the clear morning sky. Not even one cloud was visible from the window. *This will be a good beach day,* Gabby thought while observing the panoramic view from the window, still sitting in bed and drinking her first morning coffee. It was the beginning of July; the summer days here were very hot and humid. Gabby and Aaron took a long weekend and traveled together to Florida. Gabby was pleasantly surprised by this state, despite its reputation of being a place mostly for elders. The traffic on the roads was less hectic than in New York. Visibly, there were fewer people walking on the streets. She enjoyed eating fresh tropical fruits every day, trying mango and papaya for the first time; they quickly became her favorite fruits. Aaron and she savored a few local dishes at the restaurants where they dined. They enjoyed being on the beach together, as they once did when they were younger. The golden sand on Florida's East Coast beach reminded them of their beloved beaches in Varna.

A few months ago, Gabby left her friend Emma's house and moved in with Aaron. She had an honest conversation with him before she moved out. He was one of not very many people in her life whom she could share her deep thoughts and secrets with. It was reassuring to discover that, in spite of all the years apart, they had not lost the connection they once had.

Gabby shared with Aaron the truth about having feelings for her girlfriend's husband. She elucidated to Aaron the impossible situation she was in—living in her friend's house and also having feelings for Angel. The idea to move in together actually came from Aaron. He was living alone in a two-bedroom apartment and was very happy to have Gabby around. The arrangement started as an invitation for her to be his roommate. They both knew that being roommates would not last for a long time. Emma knew it as well. It was one thing to make a decision to move out, and an entirely different issue to convince Emma to see the benefits of this settlement.

Emma tried to talk her friend out of taking this step. She felt responsible for Gabby, since she was the one who insisted on her coming to the USA. She could not understand why Gabby was in such a hurry to move out. Emma and Angel let her live in their house rent-free, and they took good care of her. "Aaron is a married man, Gabby!" Emma was pleading with her. Now, when she was a wife, Emma was quite sensitive to issues she had not paid so much attention when she was younger. It was strange to hear Emma reasoning with Gabby, since Gabby had always been the one to have higher moral standards. "You are not two youngsters any more. He has responsibilities, a family, children," Emma continued.

"I have to take this step, Emma, for the sake of both of us." Gabby tried hard not to cry, and pretended that the situation was only about Aaron and her. Finally, Emma gave up and just assured her friend that if things did not work out in Gabby's favor, she would always have a place in their home. *I hope that does not happen*, Gabby told herself.

Living with Aaron was easy and comfortable, like going back as an adult to your grandmother's house. After their unexpected meeting not long ago, living together came naturally and effortlessly. Aaron was not at the apartment most of the time, since he was working diligently at the hospital. They mostly spent the weekends together, laid in bed and talked until they got tired. The two young people had lots of catching up to do, both inside and outside the bedroom. After they had their fill of making love and talking, Gabby usually cooked some of Aaron's favorite dishes, or they ate out. New York was a new town to both, and they enjoyed exploring it together.

Gabby continued going to school in the morning. With her newfound zeal, Gabby started looking for a job. Soon she found one at a pet store. Gabby fell in love with her position; it felt more like a hobby than a job. In addition to taking care of and playing with pets all day, she got an employee discount!

So Gabby was getting lots of quality products for Zoe. It was hard to separate from her beloved pet, but Zoe was Emma's cat; Gabby was just her stepmother. Gabby tried not to be selfish, but to think that it was in the animal's best interest to live in a house with a yard, rather than to be reduced to living in a small apartment.

Emma was not going to let Gabby off that easily, though. She continued to invite her friend to their house regularly. Gabby was using the distance between the two houses as an excuse not to visit. She offered instead to meet for lunch once a week; just Emma and she. Gabby was happy that she was able to stay away from Angel. Her feelings for him slowly started to subside.

Her feelings for Aaron, on other hand, were thriving. They were both more mature now. They were intuitively sensing how to deal with each other, what to say, what to spare. There were not any parents or relatives around to tell them what to do and how to feel. They could pretend for a while that they were a real couple; that Aaron did not have a family waiting for his return. Gabby knew that this idyllic situation would not last long. She felt that fortune owes her this time with him, the time that was taken away from them during their youth. She was happy, just simply happy, at this moment. She was not thinking about their future together, not making plans to be with Aaron forever. She did not give him an ultimatum to leave his family, and he did not ask her to marry him. Things were simple. They loved each other. At this moment, she had everything she needed.

The sex between them was breathtakingly beautiful. They were, however, not experiencing the same level of passion as they did during their youth. This time was different. They both know what they want, what makes them happy. Aaron was more patient with Gabby. Gabby had less unrealistic expectations about how things should be. They both worried less about their own performance, and enjoyed making the other person satisfied and happy.

Gabby was not concerned about getting pregnant this time. She had made the decision long ago to take the initiative of protecting herself, and not to rely on her partner. On the other hand, she felt stricken by the thought that it would not be the end of the world if she got pregnant. The two of them loved each other; she was approaching the age when women started thinking about getting married and starting a family. Her only fear in this situation would be that she might end up being a single parent. In this imaginary scenario, she questioned her ability to take care of a child by herself in the USA. She probably would need to return home and rely on her parents for help. This reminded her about her own childhood under the care of her grandparent. Is that what she wanted for her future child? "Gabby, stop worrying about the unborn Petko"—she chuckled at this clever Bulgarian sentence.

Gabby caught herself thinking often about returning to Bulgaria. She knew her time with Aaron was limited. When his second year of living in the USA ends, she will need to make some tough decisions. Where will she live? Could she be able to afford to live alone in New Yorck and send money to her family in Bulgaria at the same time? She had burned the bridge going back to Emma's house. And the future was unknown. There was a sort of beauty in this petrifying perception, however. One can never know what the future might hold.

Gabby chased away thoughts about the uncertainty of her future. She was here now with Aaron. The love between them was real; it was palpable. The hotel receptionist asked them when they checked in if they were newlyweds on their honeymoon. They both laughed. Later, she allowed herself to imagine how she would be feeling if this had been a real honeymoon trip.

She left the coffee cup on the nightstand and turned her attention to Aaron. He was sleeping next to her in the enormous king-size bed in the hotel room. She gently kissed his face, his lips, as he slowly opened his eyes and turned toward her. He reached out and hugged her tightly, whispering, "Dobro utro, zaharche moe" ("Good morning, my sugar thing"). He smiled at her and started tracing her body with his hot fingers. It was difficult for Gabby to hold back her cries of pleasure. The hotel room was filled with her deep moans and the smells of their sweet love-making. Later, they took a hot shower together.

During breakfast, Aaron said to her, "I am so happy that I can talk to you in Bulgarian. It feels like I have unexpectedly returned to my early years in college. I feel young and careless!"

They decided to explore some of the interesting places around Florida. A name on the map caught Gabby's attention. "Let us go to this Honeymoon Island on the West Coast. The guide says that there is a ferry to the Caladesi Island." They agreed to spend a few hours on the beach, have an early dinner and stay to watch the fireworks on the beach for the 4th of July celebration. To both, this would be their first year witnessing the celebration of Independence Day on American soil. They sat on a beach towel, hugged each other, and watched the spectacle of lights in the night sky.

The following day was the last day of their mini-vacation. They continued driving along Florida country roads that reminded them of the Bulgarian countryside, minus the tropical climate. They read in their travel guide about a small town, Cassadaga, where they were many fortune tellers. Both Gabby and Aaron were very practical people who did not believe in mediums, or paranormal events. But on that day, they experienced an unexplained impulse to drive through that town to see what would happen.

They stopped at a small, white-colored office building that looked pretty normal, sort of like a massage office. They were greeted at the front desk by an overweight middle-aged woman. Dressed in pink scrubs, she did look as if she could belong to the medical profession and explained to them what payment methods the reader was accepting. This seemed very practical to Gabby, who was expecting to see something magical as soon as she stepped through the door. After they paid, the lady informed them that the clairvoyant person would see them individually. She called for Aaron first, using his first name, which did not alert Gabby, since the credit card they paid with was in his name. After about 10 minutes he came back; his face looked pale and scared. Gabby did not have time to ask him any questions when she heard her name. *This is strange; I did not give my name to anyone here*, Gabby thought.

When she entered the dimmed room, she could not see the face of the old woman very well. She just saw that her skin was dark, which reminded Gabby of the Gypsy women in her native country. Some of them would stop you on the street to do a palm reading—if you promised to pay them. This particular Gypsy looked very calm and composed. She asked Gabby to sit down, although there was no crystal ball or deck of cards in front of her. She was looking outside the window at the small garden in the backyard.

"You came here from a great distance, my dear," the Gypsy started talking. Gabby said nothing. "You knew this man that was just here before you from a long time ago." Gabby did not confirm. "You are going to marry in the next few years, but not to him." Gabby's heart filled with sorrow. "Your husband will be a blond man with blue eyes. You will have a long and happy life together."

The Gypsy went silent for a few minutes. Gabby did not know if the session was over. She waited a few more minutes and, since the lady did not speak, Gabby stood up. "One last thing, my dear, the little doll that you have in your possession needs to be given to your daughter, the same way your mother gave it to you." Gabby could not move; she was stricken. Nobody outside her family and her close friends knew the story of the porcelain doll. She had never shared the story with Aaron, so he could not have given this information to the old woman.

Gabby did not know what to say, so she just muttered, "Thank you."

Back in the car, Aaron and she did not speak for a long time. Suddenly, he turned the car into a small, off-road place. When the motor stopped, Aaron put his head on the steering wheel and started to cry. "She told me about my Mom's death, Gabby."

Gabby took his head in her hands and started kissing his wet face. "She told me about my Mom as well," Gabby said, withholding the other important information.

During the two years they were together, Aaron and Gabby never mentioned this episode again, either to each other or in conversations with other people. Some days, Gabby wondered if she would meet and marry the man who was described, and have a daughter, as the Gypsy lady had predicted.

7

Visit to the Old Country

*"New beginnings are often disguised
as painful endings."*

– Lao Tzu (604 BC–531 BC), ancient Chinese philosopher
and writer. He is the reputed author of the *Tao Te Ching*,
the founder of philosophical Taoism, and a deity in
religious Taoism and traditional Chinese religions.

The following summer, Gabby and Emma were traveling
to Bulgaria on a short vacation. Angel was left behind by
Emma, to work. This settled Gabby's fears about spending time
with him. Aaron decided to use those few weeks to visit his
family in Israel; he had not seen them since the winter break.
Gabby had graduated from the English school for adults recently.
She was planning to take a test for English proficiency when she
came back and then look for a better-paying job.

Travelling with Emma had always been a very enjoyable
experience. Gabby realized that they were traveling on an
airplane for the first time together. In Bulgaria, in the past, they
had only taken bus, car and train rides together. Now the two

girlfriends had leisure time to talk about their shared memories and their plans for the future.

Unfortunately, on one of the flights, they were not able to get tickets for seats next to each other. Gabby was seated next to a middle-aged American man. They casually introduced themselves. He turned to be a very interesting fellow traveler; the time they spent together really broadened Gabby's horizons. The man, a journalist himself, who had traveled the world, talked and shared stories during the entire flight. He has been to lots of war zones and had the experiences Gabby had only been dreaming about. Now he was writing his memoirs.

The gentleman offered his help to Gabby about finding a job as a journalist. The young woman was impressed by his stories and astonished by his offer. Was this an act of destiny again, sending her the people she most needs at the right time? *If I had sat next to Emma, I would never have met this man*, Gabby thought. They exchanged phone numbers and email addresses. He was traveling to London, where Gabby and Emma were transferring planes to catch their flight to Sofia.

The first impression, after landing on Bulgarian soil, that both women shared was that the air in the Capital was very polluted. But this was their Homeland; they would try not to set their minds on criticizing everything around them, like some Bulgarians do after spending time abroad. Gabby, especially, was striving to be an impartial observer.

Upon arrival at Sofia's airport, the two young women were greeted by Emma's parents, who took them out for lunch, since Gabby had a few hours' wait time until her flight to Varna. Emma tried to convince her friend to stay for a few days in the

Capital. "No, Emma, I am longing to see my parents and my sisters. There is nothing in Sofia that is alluring to me. I will miss you for those few weeks, but we will be traveling back together again."

Gabby was noticing the passengers at the airport, as was her habit when traveling. What she was astounded to realize, after living a few years abroad, was that most passengers were not smiling; they looked as if they were carrying all the world's problems on their shoulders. She also recalled that the crew on the Bulgarian airplane and the staff at the airport were unexpectedly rude to their customers. This was in sharp contrast to the excellent customer service she received in the States. Was it because of the social behavior Bulgarians developed during the Communist regime when they had to hide their thoughts and disapproval of the inhumane regime? *Maybe people will slowly change and will accept different ways of living and interacting with each other,* she thought to herself.

The meeting between Gabby and her family was heartwarming. Rose hugged and kissed her daughter so many times. Bulgarian families are usually very close. Adult children visit their parents regularly, not only because of obligation, but because they truly enjoy each other's company. Rose loathes being separated from her children, especially from her first-born. Gabby being so far away brought to her mind the long-forgotten memories of separation from her daughter during Gabriella's infancy. Rose was also hoping, like most Bulgarian mothers do, that Gabby, during one of her visits, would bring along a boyfriend or a husband-to-be. She was envisioning a big wedding, and grandchildren running around. Miho was more realistic. He was simply happy that his daughter is back, healthy and doing well.

Gabby was surprised to see how fully independent her sisters had become. They had taken their own paths in life. She was also happy to spend time with her grandparents. Iona, her maternal grandmother, was still very active in her 80s. Ivan, her fraternal grandfather, was taking care of his garden as always, and still driving his old beloved car.

Gabby savored every minute of her time in Bulgaria. It was true that people appreciate their country and their loved ones after being separated from them. She was enjoying the delicious food, the beach, and her time not only with her family, but also with her childhood friends.

Gabriella realized how much life in a foreign country had changed her. She was more mature now, more patient, more accepting of differences in people. She did not share with her parents the information about meeting and living with Aaron. She knew they would not approve of her cohabiting with a married man. She had learned long ago that it is better to hide some parts of your life away from the eyes of other people, even if they are your own family.

The vacation days flew by as quickly as birds. It was time again for Gabby to say good-bye to her family. She dreams about them coming to visit her—in the future, of course, when she will settle in. As always, she prefers that her loved ones do not come to the airport with her, since she dislikes separations, tears, painful hugs. Ironically, Gabby was flying toward one of the most painful severances, one she would encounter soon— the one with Aaron.

At the Sofia Airport, she met up with Emma. Her dear friend was glowing, more beautiful than ever; the vacation had suited her well. They bought lots of newspapers and magazines to read on the plane. Both women enjoyed doing crossword puzzles. This time, they were not going to be parted during the flight and would spend lots of time together. When Gabby entered the Bulgarian airplane, she heard the familiar music and lyrics of the iconic song, "My country, my Bulgaria," which brought tears to her eyes. She turned toward Emma and saw tears in her eyes as well.

The trip back to the USA went well, without any technical difficulties, longer wait times or lost baggage. On the last part of the trip, Emma suddenly turned to Gabby and said, "Gabby, I am pregnant!"

Gabby hugged and kissed her friend. "So, Angel's last New Year's wish became true, finally!" she joked. This explained her friend's glowing face. "I am so happy for you two!" Gabby was being honest. At the same time, the thought of Emma needing her help after the child was born crossed her mind. This would mean facing Angel again. As much as Gabby was happy for her girlfriend, she recognized the need to act quickly on finding a place to live after Aaron's departure.

Aaron and Angel were both waiting for them at the New York Airport. Gabby remembered her first time arriving at the Big Apple two years ago, being scared and not knowing what was waiting for her in the new country. "Gabby, are you daydreaming again?" Aaron interrupted her thoughts. He was holding a big bouquet of flowers, and so was Angel. Emma shared the good news with Aaron, and the four of them went to the airport restaurant to celebrate, like in the old days. Aaron was looking relaxed after his vacation. He and Gabby usually do not discuss his family, so she did not ask the traditional questions. Aaron, on other hand was curious about Rose, Miho, and her sisters. Gabby sighed. They had so much history, so many memories together. They understand each other after saying even one word. Why can't they continue living as a couple? Why is life so unfair?!

A few months had passed since Gabby came back from her trip to the homeland. She had excelled at her English proficiency test and decided to take some college classes online. Her hopes were that she would be able to master the English language on a higher level. That would improve her chances of finding a better-paying job. She decided to use the time she had left with Aaron wisely, to further her education. Their relationship was better than ever. For those two years, they did not have a single argument, or disagreement. Maybe when lovers know that their time together is limited, they give each other the best of themselves.

Gabby remembered her unexpected meeting with the American journalist on her flight to London. She e-mailed him, and he responded quickly. He asked about her portfolio and said that if she did not have one, he was willing to help her build it. Gabby was moving one step closer to achieving her dream of writing, and becoming a journalist, in the USA. At that time, the technology was improving, and lots of jobs were available to be performed online from any part of the world.

Gabby was seriously contemplating moving to another state, since she could write from anywhere.

Where should she go?

Aaron actually was the one who came up with the idea of moving to Florida. Gabby had great memories of their getaway trip there, but was this a good choice of state to live in? She had some concerns about the tropical climate and the danger of hurricanes. Aaron had an old aunt who was living in Boca Raton, Florida. She needed someone young to live in her home and take care of her and was willing to pay a decent salary. The situation was perfect for Gabby! Now she would be able to earn some money, while continuing with her online classes. Eventually, she could start working at an online job.

Aaron was supposed to leave the country in November. A few months before the set-up date for the departure, Gabby started to feel forlorn. She knew that she needed to be looking at the separation from her loved one as only one episode of her life, not as a tragic event. She really needed to find some spiritual guidance at this difficult time, and found herself attracted to reading books on self-help. She was also happy to discover a Bulgarian Orthodox Church in New York and slowly started participating regularly in religious life. This gave her much-needed strength and wisdom so she would not feel abandoned. It was difficult for Emma to understand the reason behind Gabby's decision to move to another state. To her, nobody in his right mind would ever want to leave New York. And why was her best friend making the choice to go somewhere else when she has friends and a place where she could stay right here?

Gabby and Aaron decided to travel one more time to Florida together. They arrived at Fort Lauderdale Airport on this hot October day. The weather felt summery-warm, even with the cooler mornings and nights. "Aaron, look at this colorful airplane: the tail is painted in red, yellow, green and blue." Gabby was observing that parked aircraft while they were waiting to leave the crowded plane. "I think this one belongs to Cayman Airways," he said, having had more traveling experience than she. At that moment, Gabby did not know how seeing this particular airplane would predict her future life.

Aaron introduced Gabby to his Aunt Sally. The two women instantly liked each other. Sally was the widow of a banker and had no children. She had traveled the world, and was well-educated and a very refined person. Aaron was her favorite nephew; and they had built a good relationship in the last decade. He was confident that he was leaving Gabby in good hands. He truthfully told his aunt the nature of his relationship with the young Bulgarian woman.

The plan was that Gabby would stay in Aaron's apartment until the end of November so they could spend Thanksgiving together, then fly to Florida in the beginning of December.

It was difficult to separate from Aaron for the second time in her life. This time, other people had not forced them to part. The couple made the conscious decision together. *It was for the best, for all parties involved*, Gabby told herself. She was trying hard to be brave, but had a premonition that they were separating irrevocably.

They also decided to avoid a heartbreaking scene at the airport by saying good-bye at the apartment where they had spent two happy years together. Just as Aaron was about to leave, he took a small jewelry box from his pocket as he covered Gabby's face with gentle kisses. "Do not cry, my love. Maybe the good fortune or the God that you believe in will bring us together again one more time." He opened a small red box, took out elaborately made to resemble a lace, golden cross, and placed it in her hand. "I did not have a chance to say a proper good-bye last time we separated, or to give you anything. I want you to remember me every day of your life by always wearing this little symbol of my love close to your heart."

"Thank you, Aaron, I will treasure this gift as long as I live. It will be my solace," Gabby said in a tremulous voice. They kissed passionately for the last time. She slowly closed the door behind him; and with that symbolic gesture, they put an end to the passionate love story that had started in their youth.

Epilogue

The adjustment to life in Florida was much easier than Gabby's experience two years ago when she arrived in New York. She was already accustomed to American life, but this time she had to rely mostly on herself, since Emma was not around to organize every small detail of her life. Sally did not pay much attention to what Gabby did with her time, as long as she was available to drive her around a few times during the week. Sally enjoyed her weekly appointments to the hairdresser, the nail salon and the bridge games with her girlfriends. She was blessed to have healthy senior years, which she truly was enjoying. *I want to be like Sally when I get older*, Gabby thought to herself.

The most unusual aspect at the new place for Gabby was the weather. Since the temperature was very comfortable in December, she did not need to wear warm clothes and boots. Some days, she could even sunbathe at the beach during the winter months.

One of the most difficult adjustments for Gabby was the necessity of driving a car. There was neither a subway, nor reliable public transportation in Florida. To her credit, Gabby had been able to get a driving license in New York, although her driving experience was limited. She was supposed to drive Aaron's aunt around in the lady's old Buick. The first few times Gabby sat behind the wheel; she was praying constantly to arrive safely at her destination. After a few months of driving, Gabby had learned how to relax. Soon, she would even be able to enjoy her rides while listening to the car radio.

Sally was a very active lady for her age; she was, in fact, approaching 80. In her youth, she was a prominent horse rider, and told Gabby that she had won a few competitions. There were pictures around the apartment of Sally riding different horses. Now Sally chooses less dangerous sports; so, she is an avid bird-watcher and teaches Gabby about various birds through books and paintings of birds in her apartment.

Sally planned to make reservations on a cruise ship to a couple of Caribbean destinations in January, for Gabby's birthday. She was trying to cheer up her young friend, since Gabby did not feel like herself after Aaron's departure. The plan was that the two women would participate in some bird-watching activities during their vacation. Otherwise, Sally did not wish to visit the regular tourist attractions that she already had seen multiple times. She told Gabby to participate in any excursions and organized activities she liked. This discussion took place in one of the ship's luxurious restaurants during dinnertime. Gabby was truly enjoying the delicious food on the ship. She tried lobster for the first time in her life tonight, also allowing herself to indulge in wine tasting. Her spirits were indeed lifted.

The conversation with Sally was interrupted by a very handsome middle-aged man who approached their table. His hair was blond, his face encircled by well-shaped facial hair. The man introduced himself in a very old-fashioned chivalrous way by bowing politely and kissing both women's hands. He said his name was Stephan. Gabby detected a slight German accent while he was talking. She was a good judge of accents, from her experiences at the school she had attended in New York and from working with customers at the pet store there.

Sally invited Stephan to sit with them. She likes having company, especially the company of handsome younger men. It was obvious, however, that Stephan was attracted to Gabby, who recalled seeing him on the deck, observing her. She had to admit that he was a charming companion.

His presence made the atmosphere at the table much more relaxed. Stephan shared some of his life stories in a very funny way that had both of the women laughing. Sally learned that he is an engineer, and lives in New York. Gabby was not listening very carefully. She felt her head getting heavy, maybe from the wine she drank earlier. She finished her dessert and excused herself, noting the disappointed look in Stephan's eyes.

During one of the trips on land, Gabby entered an intriguing-looking souvenir shop, painted in white and blue colors. She wanted to buy some souvenirs, planning to send some to Emma, and to keep some for her relatives and friends in Bulgaria. The store was full of the usual cheaply made, but expensive-to-buy clutter. She was ready to leave when she spotted Stephan. Gabby could feel his eyes on her face. *I cannot leave now; I have to go talk to him*, she thought to herself. He invited her for a drink at an English pub that had been recommended to him by the cab driver. Gabby agreed. "Where is your aunt?" he asked.

"She is not my aunt. I work for her," Gabby laughed.

"You do look alike. I am surprised that you are not related." His words made Gabby think about the physical similarities between Sally and herself. Yes, the man was indeed a good observer. Both women have bodies with a petite build; when they smile, their faces light up in a similar way; their eyes are full of laughter and playfulness; they both have nice, thick, wavy hair; Sally's hair now is a deep gray color, while Gabby's natural dark-brown hair is untouched by artificial coloring.

It was a soft late afternoon on this Caribbean island, Cayman. Some people say that here they discovered Paradise on Earth; after all, the warm weather, the bright tropical sun, being away from the cold North and the noise of the big cities did bring to mind an idyllic picture of Eden. Dusk was just starting to settle. The prospect of sitting in the dark pub was not very appealing to Gabby anymore. She regretted that she had accepted Stephan's proposal to go out for drinks. And he, somehow sensed her remorse, quickly requesting the waiter to seat them outside, where they spent a few peaceful hours together, enjoying their drinks, marveling at the gorgeous pink colors of the sunset as it faded away over the beach, and having a nice chat about different subjects. Stephan was indeed very intelligent, and easy to talk to. Gabby was surprised to discover that she felt quite comfortable in his company. She had always been very shy and reserved with men she did not know well.

Suddenly, Stephan took out a little object from his pocket and put it carefully in Gabby's hands. Gabby was puzzled when she saw a delicate porcelain doll that was almost identical to her treasured old possession. "I bought this for you at the store today," said Stephan.

Gabby smiled with appreciation and said, "Thank you. This was very nice of you, but I already have one of these dolls. Mine is very old; it was the first toy my mom bought for me. In fact, now I see one major difference between the two: mine is a female doll, and the one you are giving me is a male."

"I guess they will make a nice couple and maybe have a family one day," Stephan said as he looked at her, his piercing deep-blue eyes full of hope. In the heat of their gaze, a new romance was born.

About the Author

Susan Jeffers Photography

Desislava Kaludova grew up in Varna, Bulgaria. She studied at Varna Medical University and became a Medical Doctor in 1995, but she had a passion for writing since early childhood. At age 32, she came to the United States with her family and a few small suitcases to start a new life. Now Desislava lives in Tampa Bay, Florida. *The Porcelain Doll* is her debut novel.